A Manual
for
Lay Eucharistic
Ministers

In the Episcopal Church

Beth Wickenberg Ely
foreword by James C. Fenhagen

MOREHOUSE PUBLISHING
HARRISBURG, PENNSYLVANIA

Copyright © 1991 Beth Wickenberg Ely

Morehouse Publishing
PO Box 1321
Harrisburg, PA 17105

Library of Congress Cataloging-in-Publication Data
Ely, Beth Wickenberg.
    A manual for lay Eucharistic ministers in the Episcopal Church / Elizabeth Wickenberg Ely.
        p.   cm.
    Includes bibliographical references.
    ISBN 0-8192-1573-2 (pbk.)
    1. Lord's Supper—Lay administration—Episcopal Church— Handbooks, manuals, etc.   I. Title.
BX5949.C5E49   1991
264'.03036—dc20   91-12433
                                                  CIP

Printed in the United States of America

10   9   8   7   6

Contents

TITLE III
CANON 3. (1994)

TITLE III
MINISTRY

CANON 3.
Of Licensed Lay Persons

Sec. 1 (a). A confirmed adult communicant in good standing may serve as Lay Reader, Pastoral Leader, Lay Preacher, Lay Eucharistic Minister, or Catechist, if licensed by the Bishop or Ecclesiastical Authority of the Diocese in which the person is a member. Guidelines for training and selection of such persons shall be established by the Bishop.

(b). The Presiding Bishop or the Suffragan Bishop for the Armed Forces may license a member of the Armed Forces to exercise one or more of these ministries in the Armed Forces in accordance with the provisions of this Canon.

Sec. 2 (a). A license shall be given only at the request and upon the recommendation of the Member of the Clergy in charge of the Congregation in which the person will be serving. The license shall be issued for a period of time not to exceed three years and shall be revocable by the Bishop, or upon the request of the Member of the Clergy in charge of the Congregation.

(b). Renewal of the license shall be determined on the basis of the acceptable performance of the ministry by the licensee and upon the endorsement of the Member of the Clergy in charge of the Congregation in which the person is serving.

(c). A person licensed in any Diocese under the provisions of this Canon may serve in another Congregation in the same or another Diocese at the invitation of the Member of the Clergy in charge, and with the consent of the Bishop in whose jurisdiction the service will occur.

(d). The person licensed shall conform to the directions of the Bishop and the Member of the Clergy in charge of the Congregation in which the person is serving, in all matters relating to the conduct of services, the sermons to be read, and the dress to be worn. In every respect, the person licensed shall conform to the requirements and limitations set forth in the rubrics and other directions of the Book of Common Prayer.

Sec. 5 (a). A Lay Eucharistic Minister is a person licensed to this extraordinary ministry. The Lay Eucharistic Minister shall have one or both of the following functions, as specified in the license:

(1). Administering the elements at any Celebration of Holy Eucharist in the absence of a sufficient number of Priests or Deacons assisting the celebrant:

(2). Directly following a Celebration of the Holy Eucharist on Sunday or other Principal Celebrations, taking the Sacrament consecrated at the Celebration to members of the Congregation who, by reason of illness or infirmity, were unable to be present at the Celebration.

(b). Qualifications, requirements, and guidelines for the selection, training, and use of Lay Eucharistic Ministers shall be established by the Bishop.

(c). This ministry is not to take the place of the ministry of Priests and Deacons in the exercise of their office, including regular visitation of members unable to attend the Celebration of the Holy Eucharist. A Lay Eucharistic Minister should normally be under the direction of a Deacon of the Congregation, if there be one.

Foreword

Beth Ely's A *Manual for Lay Eucharistic Ministers in the Episcopal Church* is a remarkable blending of theological insight, practical wisdom and personal experience. As the author notes in her Introduction, the book was conceived in response to a practical need and then developed as an Honors Thesis in the area of Practical Theology. It was my privilege to serve as encourager, critic and mentor throughout the writing of the thesis and then see its adaptation for use throughout the church at large. Its value as a training manual lies not only in the practical assistance it offers to Lay Eucharistic Ministers and those responsible for their training and support but also for its concise development of a sound theology of the eucharist which could be used by anyone seeking to learn more about the church's central act of worship.

In St. Paul's Epistle to the Colossians there is a magnificent testimony to the interconnectedness of the people of God which I believe underlies the vision that this manual embodies. "(Jesus Christ) is before all things," writes Paul "and in him all things hold together" (1:17). It is the living out of this fundamental interconnectedness that makes the ministry of the Lay Eucharistic Minister so important in the life of the church. We no longer see the church as a community gathered around a Minister, but a community of many ministries gathered around the Lord. As the people of God we gather for worship and then scatter into the various places where we live out our lives as signs of the presence of Christ to others. When a member of the laity is sent forth from the parish church bearing the sacrament as a representative of the gathered community to connect with scattered members of the Body who cannot be present, we are incarnating the very nature of the church itself. The Christian church refers not only to a building or to people gathered for worship, but to a community of people who are both gathered and scattered while, at the same time, profoundly interconnected by the Risen Christ who binds them together. The Lay Eucharistic Minister is a sign of the priesthood of all believers to which all baptized Christians are called. This understanding of the church is central to the recovery of the church's mission in our day and is reflected in every word Beth Ely writes.

In the canon that establishes the Lay Eucharistic Minister as an authorized ministry within the gathered church, the following words are used to signify its importance: "A Lay Eucharistic Minister is a person licensed to this extraordinary ministry." Beth Ely's manual provides the educational resource we need to honor what 'extraordinary implies, by giving the Lay Eucharistic Minister an understanding of the importance of what he or she is called to be, and by linking this ministry into that long tradition by which we "although many" continue to be "one Body in Christ" and able throughout our lives to "dwell in Him and He in us." Beth Ely has given us a little book that is packed full of wisdom. May it be used far and wide.

James C. Fenhagen
Chelsea Square, Lent 1991

The Communion

Blind and alone she sat on her bed
and sang
an old hymn
from an old church.

She sang for herself.

Her sound came from somewhere
deep in her being,
to sing was her need.

Her needing made me stop.

And somewhere between her singing
and my stopping
something happened
that had never happened to me
before.

I entered her room.

I said in the faulted Spanish:
I come with God
with Jesucristo
for you.

And she shook into tears.

I come with the Holy Communion
El Cuerpo
de Jescristo
pro tu.

*She began to nod
and her blind, closed eyes wept.*

*Somehow her desire had reached
me and the surprise and joy
could not be contained in words or smiles.*

And she said: I was so alone.

*And I said: Jesucristo has come;
I have come;
and I held her
and tried to talk
but we were beyond words.* *

*Reprinted from *Images: Women in Transition*, compiled by Janice Grana, poem by Catharine Stewart Roache. (Winona, MN: Saint Mary's Press, 1977.) Used by permission of the publisher. All rights reserved.

Introduction

THE FIRST CANON IN THE EPISCOPAL CHURCH that allowed lay people to take the eucharist immediately after the Sunday service to ill and infirm members of their congregation was passed by the 1985 General Convention. That canon used the title "Lay Eucharistic Minister" to define those who (1) administered the chance during worship services when not enough clergy were available and (2) took communion to the sick. After the first experiences with these two ministries, however, many people began to realize that different skills and gifts were required of each. Subsequently, in most places only those who took eucharist to sick or infirm parishioners became known as Lay Eucharistic Ministers or LEMs, pronounced as 3 letters ell-ee-em, not like "lem," which reminds one oddly of lemmings. The term Chalice Bearer was reserved for lay people who administer the communion in church. The 1988 revision of the original canon also helped to clarify this further. In 1994, modification helped resolve the question of *when* this ministry could take place. This manual is for those lay people who are called and licensed to minister to the ill and infirm in their congregations by taking them the eucharist directly after regularly scheduled services.

In passing the Lay Eucharistic Ministers' canon in 1985, the General Convention recognized the diversity of dioceses in this country. Some, such as Idaho and Iowa, are rural dioceses; some, such as New York, have large urban populations; some, such as Los Angeles, have many members who live in suburbs; and some dioceses are a mixture of all three. Each has needs particular to its situation. For example, parishioners in a rural diocese may not live close to the church or to each other. In that situation, more LEMs may be needed to cover a wide geographical area. In an urban diocese, however, LEMs may need to go in pairs if their physical safety is an issue. In a suburban setting, dioceses may need to train their LEMs to minister to people they may not know well because of the transience of the area. Needs of dioceses will be different because of geography, population shifts, the particular blend of ages, backgrounds and needs of parishioners, and many other factors. Therefore, this canon specifies that the "qualifications, requirements, and guidelines for the selection, training, and use of Lay Eucharistic Ministers" be set by the bishop of each diocese.[1]

What those bishops have decided, often in consultation with their diocesan liturgy committees, has led to vast differences in the training and utilization of LEMs around the country. Some dioceses do not use LEMs at all. Some sponsor LEM training programs several times a year. Others leave the training to individual clergy, only specifying certain areas of study.

When I began to train a group of Lay Eucharistic Ministers at Grace Episcopal Church in Charleston, S.C., in the summer of 1988—three years after the canon was passed—I was dismayed to find no information available from the national Episcopal Church to help me. Therefore, I was compelled to gather my own information without a major theological library at my disposal and without adequate time to thoroughly investigate each area of study.

In pursuing what I perceive to be a gap in the church's encouragement and implementation of this canon, I have taken an informal survey of every diocese of the Episcopal Church within the fifty states. Out of almost one hundred dioceses, nearly sixty replied with information on what kind of training, if any, they are offering their LEMS. Some dioceses have thorough training programs in place, but the majority do not. Many expressed frustration similar to my own and great interest in my project, hoping that my information might give them a foundation on which to build their long-delayed LEM training programs.

This manual is a result of extensive research into those areas I judge crucial to an LEM's training, as well as nearly ten years of experience in local congregations. The book provides not only theological, historical, liturgical, and pastoral information but also practical hints for the Lay Eucharistic Minister. It covers areas of information not required by some dioceses and does not cover areas mandatory in others. Indeed, local situations and usage should and will continue to vary.

What began as an attempt to train LEMs soon became an honors thesis at the General Theological Seminary, thoughtfully guided by the Very Reverend James C. Fenhagen, Dean of the seminary, and the Reverend J. Neil Alexander, Assistant Professor of liturgy, and lovingly supported by my husband, Duncan Cairnes Ely.

This manual is written for all Lay Eucharistic Ministers carrying the Body and Blood of Christ to their brothers and sisters in such wide-ranging places as New York City, Anchorage, and suburban Chicago, as well as to every other home, hospital bed, and nursing facility in between. God bless you all in your extraordinary ministry.

The Reverend Beth Wickenberg Ely
Episcopal Church of the Advent
Spartanburg, South Carolina

November 4, 1996

Acknowledgments

Many thanks to the following dioceses who responded to my informal survey: Alaska, Arizona, Arkansas, Atlanta, California, Central Gulf Coast, Central New York, Central Pennsylvania, Colorado, Connecticut, Delaware, Eau Claire, East Tennessee, Eastern Oregon, Easton, El Camino Real Florida, Fond du Lac, Fort Worth, Georgia, Hawaii, Indianapolis, Kentucky, Lexington, Long Island, Louisiana, Maine, Maryland, Massachusetts, Michigan, Minnesota, Mississippi, Montana, New Hampshire, New York, North Dakota, Northeast Texas, Northwestern Pennsylvania, Oklahoma, Quincy, Rhode Island, Rochester, South Dakota, Southern Virginia, Southwestern Virginia, Springfield, Texas, Vermont, Virginia, Washington, West Tennessee, West Texas, Western Kansas, Western Louisiana, Western Massachusetts, and Western Oregon.

Chapter 1

Custom and Canon:
The History of Lay Administration
of the Eucharist

Legacy from the Earliest Christians

IN THE EARLY YEARS OF THE CHURCH, lay Christians regularly ministered to the ill and dying by taking them the eucharist. This was a time before the clerical orders of ministry—bishops, priests, and deacons—came into being as they are today. The work of the church was much more fluid when congregations were still relatively small and close together and under persecution.

Early Christian writers tell about what seems to have been a regular practice: The laity took the sacrament home from the Sunday service. During the following week they would communicate themselves and their families and perhaps administer communion to the sick, the shut-in, and the dying.

About the year 200, Hippolytus, a bishop in Rome, gives the earliest known picture of the laity carrying the sacrament to the widows and the sick.

> In time of need the deacon shall be diligent in giving the blessed bread to the sick. If there is no presbyter to give out what is to be distributed, the deacon shall pronounce the thanksgiving and shall supervise those who carry it away, to make sure that they attend to their duty and [properly] distribute the blessed food; the distributors must give it to the widows and the sick. Whoever is

entrusted with the duty by the church must distribute it on the same day; if he does not, he must [at least] do so on the next day. . . For [it is not his own property]; it is given him only [in trust] as bread for the poor.[2]

In the fourth century, the historian Eusebius relates a story of the dying Serapion, who asked his grandson to get him a priest. Because the priest was too ill to come, the boy communicated his grandfather just before he died.[3] A century later, the lay woman Melania the Younger is said to have taken the eucharist to a sick uncle's bedside and given him communion there three times before death.[4]

As time went on, however, persecutions ceased, and the church grew and began to need structures to govern its life and worship. One of these concerns was to regulate the laity's handling of holy elements. This need came into conflict with one of the primary concerns of the church, however: that the eucharist always be available to a dying person. It was with that in mind that people kept it in their homes as well as carried it with them when they went on long and dangerous journeys.

The conflict of these two values is foreshadowed by the very different opinions of two men who lived in the late fourth century, Ambrose and Jerome. Ambrose, Bishop of Milan, recognized the need for having the eucharist always available in case of danger or sudden death when a priest was not present. Using a story about his brother, he illustrates this view and the fact that the eucharist was readily available to the laity. Once when shipwrecked, Satyrus asked some lay people on board for the sacrament, tied it around his neck in a napkin, and leapt into the sea, entrusting his life to God. For his faith, Ambrose says, Satyrus was rescued.[5]

Jerome, however, was concerned that people would take the eucharist at home when they were not prepared to receive it in church in public worship. He wrote that communion at the eucharist is the sign of communion with the church, its beliefs, and its behavior. Therefore, "what is allowed in church is not allowed at home."[6]

In later centuries, Jerome's warnings began to take shape in increasingly strict legislation against lay people reserving the eucharist and giving communion to the sick. Throughout the first thousand years of the church, however, home reservation of the eucharist and lay communion of the sick and dying persisted, despite the attempts of local councils and synods to regulate it.

For example, in his sixth-century *Dialogues,* Pope Gregory the Great ends his story of the life of the abbot Benedict of Nursia with a story that Benedict administered the eucharist to himself in the monastery chapel just before his death.[7] In his *Ecclesiastical History* a century later, Bede gives several portraits of lay people administering the eucharist to the dying.[8]

Beginning in the late seventh century, however, stronger attempts began to be made to keep the laity from acting as ministers of the eucharist. At the Council of Trullo in about 690, legislation was passed forbidding laity to distribute communion when a bishop, priest, or deacon was available.[9] A local council at Rouen around 650 cautioned the clergy to put the sacrament in the mouth of the laity, not in their hands, probably in an effort to keep people from taking it home.[10]

The continued tension between custom and canon is made clear in eighth-century documents. A handbook of penance known as the *Penitential of Bede* encourages the faithful to carry the eucharist with them if they are going any distance or on a dangerous trip.[11] At the same time, people like Hincmar of Rheims[12] and Regino of Prum urged priests not to neglect their responsibilities of visiting the ill and taking them the eucharist. Regino was concerned that some presbyters hold the divine mysteries in such careless disregard that they hand over the holy body of the Lord to lay men and women to take to the sick . . . The presbyter himself should communicate the sick."[13]

During the eighth century, priests were becoming the usual ministers of the eucharist, taking over that task from bishops. The ordination rites of priests that included the anointing of the ordinand's hands spread in popularity, giving the impression of binding the priest's hands to the eucharist and, by implication, excluding its handling by the unordained.[14]

There still is evidence, however, that in some areas, the laity were taking the elements home and to the sick. In fact, in 931, Ratherius, Bishop of Verona, passed an edict directing the clergy not to give the eucharist to the laity for that purpose.[15]

The split between clergy and laity continued to widen considerably through the Middle Ages. In principle, however, the church seemed to recognize that in emergencies, the laity could be ministers of communion. In 1138, a council at Westminster approved the following canon: "We decree that the body of Christ be taken to the ill only by a priest or deacon; but in case of pressing necessity it may be taken, with greatest reverence by anyone."[16]

Not long thereafter in England, however, the church was forbidding even *deacons* to carry the elements to the sick. The reason for these restrictions against deacons and laity handling the eucharist probably is more disciplinary than theological. It is not a question of the theology of lay ministers of communion but an attempt to discipline priests neglecting their pastoral duties to the sick and dying.[17] A legislation passed by the Diocese of York reveals this concern:

> Presbyters should diligently visit the sick on all Sundays and festivals . . . Nor should they, as scene have presumed heretofore, send deacons with the eucharist to the sick, while they [the presbyters] devote themselves to drinking or other delights of the flesh.

The presbyters should personally go to the sick and solicitously hear their confessions.[18]

Though the ordained clergy gradually became the ordinary ministers of the eucharist, exceptions continued to be allowed and provided for by church law. "Throughout history . . . there have been special ministers, official or unofficial who brought the bread of life to those who would otherwise have died without it."[19] In modern times, the church has begun to look at lay ministry in a different light, trying to recover its roots and reexamine its theology of ministry.

The Roman Catholic Church

The acceptance and regulation of lay ministers of the eucharist in the Episcopal Church has been shaped to some extent by the Roman Catholic Church, which has allowed what it calls Extraordinary Ministers of Communion since the Vatican 11 reforms in the 1970s.

The first hint that the Roman Catholic Church was going to cast off the custom to which it had clung since the Middle Ages and allow the laity to administer the eucharist came in the document *Fidei Custos* sent to local bishops in the late 1960s. In discussing matters related to the eucharist, it said "local ordinaries may designate, or permit pastors to designate some men and women as extraordinary ministers of communion within the confines of their own jurisdiction."[20] Clearly, this ministry was meant to complement the ministries of priests, deacons, acolytes, and lectors.

Then in January 1973, the Congregation for the Disciphne of Sacraments issued the far-reaching instruction *Immensae Caritatis,* which laid the pastoral and theological framework for

Extraordinary Ministers of Communion. It read, ". . . provision must be made lest reception [of the eucharist] became impossible or difficult owing to a lack of a sufficient number of ministers."[21] These cases would include the following: when a priest is ill; when the distance to the sick or dying is too great, when the congregation at Mass is large; when there are too many sick and shut-in people for which the priest must care; when a priest has conflicting pastoral duties; or when there is no priest at all available.

Immensae Catitatis also secondarily was concerned that "the faithful who are in a state of grace and who with an upright and pious disposition, wish to share in the Sacred Banquet, may not be deprived of this sacramental help and consolation."[22] This, or course, is the primary concern of the Episcopal Church, which is not facing the clergy shortage that the Roman Catholic Church is facing.

Thus, the Roman Catholics paved the way for the Episcopal Church to begin to recover its ancient roots by enabling the laity to administer the eucharist to the sick and the dying. The Anglican Church of Canada and the Church of England, as well now have lay ministers in this capacity, as do the Evangelical Lutheran Church in America and the Lutheran Church in Canada.

The Episcopal Church

As in the Roman Catholic Church, the Episcopal Church has not recovered this vital lay ministry overnight. The process has been a long, slow one, through many steps—Lay Reader to Chalice Bearer and finally to Lay Eucharistic Minister. Along the way, each lay ministry has had to be separated out of a previous form of lay ministry. For example, a Chalice Bearer once was required to be a Licensed Lay Reader.

The first canon regarding lay liturgical ministries in the Episcopal Church was passed in 1804. It said that if no priest was available, worship could be conducted by a candidate for holy orders. But the candidate could do no part of the service assigned to the priest, including distributing the eucharist. He also only could preach a sermon written by a clergyman. The 1871 General Convention allowed lay men to do this, and in 1904, the first legislation regarding Licensed Lay Readers was passed. These men, who were in charge of parishes with no priest, also could preach with a license from the bishop.

Ninety years after the first man was licensed as a lay reader, women were allowed to perform the task though not with the same rights as men until 1969.

In 1967, Licensed Lay Readers were the first lay people in the Episcopal Church to be allowed to serve the chalice during Holy Communion, but they had to get special permission. At the time, the church still was struggling to define and differentiate the separate lay ministries. Administering the cup was considered a part of the ministry of a Lay Reader, although this particular ministry, now known as Chalice Bearer, was first proposed at the 1931 General Convention. Those known today as Lay Eucharistic Ministers are very recent in the history of the Episcopal Church. They came into being at the 1985 General Convention, after being narrowly rejected at the prior convention in 1982, where it also was proposed that Chalice Bearers be separated from Lay Readers and not be required to undergo the same training. The canon providing for Lay Eucharistic Ministers with their own specialized training passed the 1985 Convention as part of a restructuring of the Title III canons. These also introduced the church to other new lay liturgical ministers—including Lay Preachers and Lay Catechists.

The 1988 General Convention honed the canons, making more explicit the difference between the ministries of a Lay

Eucharistic Minister and a Chalice Bearer and requiring a separate license for both ministries. The rediscovery of the importance of lay ministries is an ongoing revelation in today's Episcopal Church.

Chapter 2

What Is a Lay Eucharistic Minister?

Institution or Community?

IN THE LAST FIFTY YEARS, the church has begun to reexamine and redefine itself, moving away from the legacy of the Middle Ages that perceived the church as an institution. In moving away, however, the church has come full circle, back to the first Christians. Like them, many modern Christians have come to perceive the church as community—a community of people united by their faith in Jesus Christ. Wherever that community gathers, whether inside a cathedral or church building or in a hospital room or forest, there exists the church. The church is

> no longer to be seen initially or primarily . . . as a juridically, hierarchically constituted society which exists to communicate the grace of redemption to all mankind [sic]. Rather, it is first and foremost a community of people on [a] march [through] history, a pilgrim people, the very People of God.[23]

Representing the Body

Lay Eucharistic Ministry is a vital step in helping embody and emphasize the reality of the church as community. As a person called to be a Lay Eucharistic Minister (LEM), you become an important pastoral and sacramental expression of that community. Pastorally, LEMs represent the church to those they visit by being living reminders that the sick and infirm are integral parts of that community, which is the Body of Christ. But, not only do you represent Christ's Body, the church; you also bear his Body and Blood, Christ's gifts to humanity. This is one of the main sacramental expressions of Lay Eucharistic Ministry.

Because of this, your visit to a person is never merely your own visit. In a symbolic way, you carry the parish with you as a sign of the whole community's care, support, and concern for its sick and infirm. The eucharist is the work of the whole Christian community. You are its representative; you are the Body of Christ moving outward to include all its members. The circle of the faithful is opened to those people who cannot worship with their congregation at its main celebrations.

Not only does the eucharist unite us to Christ, but it also unites us to other members of Christ's Body, too. You are a Christ-bearer used by God to connect those you visit to the larger Body of Christ in the church and in the world in the past, present, and future. Since the Christian community is bound together and strengthened through the common eucharistic meal, it is important for people not able to be there to be included into the oneness of the community. "We are not saved in isolation. We are saved as a people. What we do for the Body, which is the church, is related to our holiness and salvation."[24] As the Diocese of Oklahoma says in its manual for Lay Eucharistic Ministers,

> To be a family within the household of faith means that we must pay attention to those who are missing the communication, support, interaction and corporate worship of the whole body through no fault of their own.
>
> . . . The potential for helping the lonely, burdened, ill, dying, handicapped members of the flock to feel that they are loved, supported, and remembered as a part of the church family is unparalleled.[25]

Unresolved Issues

Because the concept of church-as-community is still being worked out theologically, many problems have yet to be resolved in areas where they conflict with the strong tradition of the church-as-institution. This can be seen most clearly in two areas: the definition of ministry and its related questions about the "right" of a layperson to carry the sacrament to the ill and infirm.

Ordinary or Extraordinary?

With the movement from thinking about church-as-institution to church-as-community has come the necessity for reexamining the roles of the clergy and the laity who make up that community. Previously, the term *minister* was used most commonly to refer to those who were ordained—the people who supposedly did "ministry" on behalf of the members of the church who are the laity. That, however, is changing. In stating in the 1979 *Book of Common Prayer* that the "ministers of the church are lay persons, bishops, priests, and deacons,"[26] the Episcopal Church is reaffirming

> an ancient Christian insight: ministry is the ordinary mode of life, for *all* Christians. It is neither exceptional nor extraordinary, all believers are called by baptism to carry on the service *(diakonia)* of Jesus who was priest not by virtue of any ordination but in virtue of his self-offering on the cross.[27]

Why then, does the canon for Lay Eucharistic Ministers describe this ministry as "extraordinary"? The reference to "extraordinary" is confusing because the church has said that *ministry* is not an ordained phenomenon. What *is* extraordinary, however, is the ministry of the laity at the eucharist in handling the elements—because, for the last thousand years or so, only deacons, priests, and bishops have shared this ministry.

But the laity and the clergy alike have been baptized into the priesthood of all believers, of people set apart. "But you are a chosen race, a royal priesthood, a holy nation, God's own people, that you may declare the wonderful deeds of him who called you out of darkness into his marvelous light" (1 Pet. 2:9). Even after they are ordained, those in the clergy remain a part of the laity *(laos)* or people of God. Our redefinition of the ministers of the church now means that the clergy are not and need not be the solitary sacramental laborers any longer. The laity can take their rightful place, not above or below those who are ordained but beside them.

> The ultimate theological source of collegiality in ministry is . . . the single baptismal vocation common to all Christians. No matter how high a view one may have about the ontological nature and effects of ordination, what binds Christians together in life and ministry is deeper than what separates or distinguishes them. Plunged into the death and rising of Jesus, all the baptized share corporate responsibility for preaching the gospel, serving those in need, and worshipping the Father in spirit and truth.[28]

Substituting for the Clergy?

There are those who disagree that baptism gives all people a right to be ministers of the sacrament. Even though there are LEMs in most parts of the Episcopal Church, there are still those that have not had the theological issues settled to their satisfaction.

When considering the passage of the canon in General Convention, much of the debate centered on the concern that the laity would somehow take away the clergy responsibilities for consecrating and administering the sacraments and providing care for their congregations. The question was whether Lay Eucharistic Ministry would become a substitute for the ministry of the clergy—especially priests and deacons. Deacons are called to a ministry of service. LEMs also are called to serve in a special way, a way that only the laity can provide. Only they can represent the Body of Christ to other lay people as a symbol of the community's care and concern for each other. This could be seen as an *extension* of the deacon's work rather than as a *substitute* for it. Consequently, LEMs generally are placed under a deacon's supervision when there is one in a parish.[29] Some dioceses will not use LEMS, however, because they still feel a conflict with the deacon's traditional calling.

Another concern is more ancient. In the early church, many lay Christians took the bread and wine to the sick and infirm members of their communities. But as the church became more structured and the functions of deacons, priests, and bishops became more defined, there was concern that by allowing the laity to continue this practice, priests would become lazy and not live up to their vows to care for their people by ministering to the sick and infirm. Therefore, by the Middle Ages, the right of lay people to do this was strictly curtailed, except in emergencies.

The same sort of concern was voiced in modern times in the debate about whether the Episcopal Church would begin to make use of Lay Eucharistic Ministers. That concern is addressed directly by the canon, which states, "This ministry is not to take the place of the ministry of Priests and Deacons in the exercise of their office, including regular visitation of members unable to attend the Celebration of the Holy Eucharist."[30]

Practically speaking, it is easy to see how LEMs can help the ordained people of the parish in ministering to the sick and infirm. If the congregation is too large for the clergy to visit as often as they would wish, if the clergy are ill or if a congregation is without sufficient clergy, this vital ministry of visiting and communicating the sick need not come to a stop, because in many places LEMs are available to help. The sacramental ministry of the community is shared more evenly between the different orders of ministry.

It is crucial to remember, however, that the laity are coequal ministers of the church along with their ordained brothers and sisters. Their ministry has value in its own right. To view it only as an extension or substitution for the ministry of bishops, priests, and deacons or only as an enhancement or support of them is to devalue and denigrate lay ministry. By their faithful service, Lay Eucharistic Ministers are showing forth the diversity of gifts given to all the people of God, lay and ordained. "Now there are varieties of gifts, but the same Spirit, and there are varieties of service, but the same Lord, and there are varieties of working, but it is the same God who inspires them all in every one. To each is given the manifestation of the Spirit for the common good" (1 Cor. 12:4-7).

Commissioning

St. Paul also says that gifts are given "to equip the saints for the work of ministry, for building up the body of Christ" (Eph. 4:12). We all are called to holiness, but the LEM "has an added opportunity and challenge in the task of building up the Body of Christ by ministering the Bread of Life. If the end . . . of the Eucharist is the unity of the Church, their ministry is at the very heart of the Church's life . . . They enter into the very action of Christ who builds His Church through the spirit."[31]

Most dioceses and parishes have chosen to mark this ministry "at the very heart of the church's life" with a commissioning service for their LEMS. The Standing Liturgical Commission has not come up with a model commissioning service, and dioceses and parishes use a wide variety. Many seem to be patterning theirs on the forms found in the *Book of Occasional Services 1994* (p.227) under the chapter entitled "Commissioning for Lay Ministries in the Church," modifying the selection for "Those Who Administer the Sacraments." Some parishes also have used "A Form of Commitment to Christian Service" found on page 420 of the Prayer Book, as well as combining it with the one from *Occasional Services.* Others add "The Renewal of Baptismal Vows" found on page 292 of the *Book of Common Prayer* in the Easter Vigil service. (For examples of commissioning services for LEMs see appendix 7.)

If baptism gives an LEM his or her primary authority for this particular ministry, why are many LEMs also commissioned at a public service? Commissioning asks a special blessing on LEMs and "gives a certain quality to the ministry which distinguishes it from the common offices of [all] lay persons."[32] Commissionings are not ordinations involving imposition of hands, transfer of ritual objects, or special clothing. They do not confer any new power. The rites of commissioning are celebrations of Word, prayer, and blessing. Their purpose is to publicly present those Lay Eucharistic Ministers appointed for this particular ministry to the faithful. Commissioning also holds up this ministry to the congregation as a reminder that it is available in times of need.

Conclusion

It is clear that the use of LEMs is not to replace the clergy's ministry of visitation but to provide a way to include the ill and infirm members of the congregation in the weekly celebration of the eucharist. That is the basic principle behind Lay Eucharistic Ministry—to make the eucharist widely available. What is at stake is not so much the rights of ministers, lay and ordained, but the need of Christians to participate fully in the eucharist through the sacrament. Lay Eucharistic Ministers are the way the Holy Spirit is guiding the modern church to provide for this need. This principle was an ancient one that gave rise to the practice in the first place in the early church and was circumscribed by priests' neglect of their duties in the Middle Ages. Our final concern should be those people who originally moved the church to action—those not able to attend the regular eucharistic assembly.

Chapter 3

The Gifts of God for the People of God

The Roots of the Holy Eucharist

The Holy Eucharist has its foundation in two forms of Jewish worship: services in the synagogue and family meals around the dinner table. Jesus was a Jew and as such was educated in all of the very structured Jewish liturgical rites. These same rites can help explain some of Jesus actions at the Last Supper.[33]

Synagogue worship consisted of readings from the Law and the Prophets (called the Old Testament by Christians), prayers, a sermon, and the faith statement of Judaism: the *Shema,* which is the basis for what Christians know as the first and great commandment quoted by Jesus (Matt. 22:37-38). The *Shema* says, "Hear, O Israel: The Lord our God is one Lord, and you shall love the Lord your God with all your heart, and with all your soul, and with all your might" (Deut. 6:4-5).

The earliest Christians were familiar with synagogue services, and most worshiped there until they were expelled before the end of the first century after Christ. These first Christians then were forced to form their own worship. There are written accounts that they did so as early as the second and third centuries, but they continued to base a part of their services on what was familiar to them from the synagogue. We still use this form with its roots in the synagogue in Morning and Evening Prayer and to a lesser extent in the part of the eucharist called "The Word of God."[34] Lay Eucharistic Ministers continue this tradition in their rite with the sections that include the collect of the day, the gospel and other passages of scripture, comments about the sermon, prayers, and the confession and declaration of forgiveness (see appendices 1 and 2).

The Jewish people also had another form of worship, one that took place around the dinner table with family or a group of friends. These meals were celebrated on the Sabbath and during great religious festivals such as Passover. At the start of the meal the head of the family took bread, gave thanks, broke it, and distributed it to everyone. At the end of the meal, he took a cup of wine and said a longer blessing over it, giving thanks for God's love, God's mighty acts in history and for the special occasion being celebrated. Everyone drank from the one cup. This was called the cup of thanksgiving or cup of blessing. The Greek word for thanksgiving is *eucharistia*, which is the same term St. Paul uses in 1 Cor. 11:23-25, the earliest written biblical account of what took place at the Last Supper. Paul's First Letter to the Corinthians was written about A.D. 55, before the more familiar accounts of the Last Supper in the gospels.

The Acts of the Apostles, written about A.D. 85, also gives a glimpse of what the earliest eucharists were like. It says that the first Christians broke tradition with the Jewish people, whose Sabbath was from sundown Friday to sundown Saturday. The early Christians gathered for worship and for breaking of bread within the setting of a meal on the first day of the week (Sunday) because that was the day of the Resurrection (Acts 20:7). By the end of the first century, however, persecution forced the meals to be separated from the eucharist proper, probably because it was too risky to meet that long in secret.

The Meaning of the Holy Eucharist

The richest treasure trove of Christian tradition belongs to the mystery of the Holy Eucharist. Theologians and scholars throughout the centuries have delved into its fathomless depths and still not exhausted the meaning of this incredible gift from God through Christ. Certainly no one ever will be able to completely comprehend the eucharist, because not only are its riches and layers of meaning infinite, but they are different for each of us each time we partake. One of the greatest mysteries of the eucharist is that it can be at the same time as intensely corporate as it is intensely personal. Liturgical scholar Dom Gregory Dix attempts to describe some of the variety of circumstances in which the eucharist has given meaning to the lives of Christians throughout history.

At the heart of [Christian worship] is the eucharistic action, a thing of absolute simplicity—the taking, blessing, breaking and giving of bread, and the taking, blessing and giving of a cup of wine and water, as these were first done with their new meaning by a young Jew before and after supper with His friends on the night before He died . . . He had told His friends to do this henceforward with the new meaning "for the *anamnesis*" [recalling] of Him, and they have done it always since.

Was ever another command so obeyed? For century after century, spreading slowly to every continent and country and among every race on earth, this action has been done, in every conceivable human circumstance, for every conceivable human need from infancy and before it to extreme old age and after it, from the pinnacles of earthly greatness to the refuge of fugitives in the caves and dens of the earth. Men have found no better thing than this to do for kings at their crowning and for criminals going to the scaffold, for armies in triumph or for a bride and bridegroom in a little country church; for the proclamation of a dogma or for a good crop of wheat; for the wisdom of the Parliament of a mighty nation or for a sick old woman afraid to die; for a schoolboy sitting at an examination or for Columbus setting out to discover America; for the famine of whole provinces or for the soul of a dead lover, in thankfulness because my father did not die of pneumonia; for a village headman much tempted to return to fetish because the yams had failed; because the Turk was at the gates of Vienna; for the repentance of Margaret; for the settlement of a strike; for a son for a barren woman; for Captain so-and-so, wounded and prisoner of war, while the lions roared in the nearby amphitheater; on the beach at Dunkirk, while the hiss of scythes in the thick June grass came faintly through the windows of the church; tremulously, by an old monk on the fiftieth anniversary of his vows; furtively, by an exiled bishop who had hewn timber all day in a prison camp near Murmansk; gorgeously, for the canonization of S. Joan of Arc—one could fill many pages with the reasons why men [and women] have done this, and not tell a hundredth part of them. And best of all, week by week and month by month, on a hundred thousand successive Sundays, faithfully, unfailingly, across all the parishes of Christendom, the pastors have done this just to *make* the *plebs sancta Dei*—the holy common people of God.[35]

The 1979 *Book of Common Prayer* restores an ancient idea that the Holy Eucharist is "the principal act of Christian worship on the Lord's Day and other major Feasts."[36] This certainly was believed by the earliest Christians. But as time went on, lay people began to receive Holy Communion less and less frequently. Eventually, it became common during some periods for lay Christians to take the eucharist once in their lifetime, on their death bed. Today, though, we once again recognize the significance of regular eucharistic participation and again are able to see that Holy Eucharist is the foundation of the corporate prayer of the church. It summons all baptized people to share in the Lords Table. Our unity in baptism is cemented through the bread and wine when we join around the table as the holy family of God. The Prayer of Consecration said by the priest expresses that unity when it asks that "we, and all others who shall be partakers of this Holy Communion, may . . . be . . . made one body with him, that he may dwell in us, and we in him."[37] God becomes present to us in the elements of the gathered Body of Christ.

> The Eucharist creates a *presence*. A presence in *time* . . . between the past of the cross and the future of our heavenly glory, a presence in space, also, that is a presence *perceptible* to our bodily senses: but more than perceptible, it is a *physical* and *real* presence, which lets us receive the actual body of the Lord. And because this risen body is the nucleus of the new world (new creation) it brings about a collective presence, in which we meet in Christ his whole body, which is the Church . . . this sacrament contains the *sacrifice* of Christ his sacrifice which is ours as well, . . . an *enduring presence.*[38]

With its links to Christ and his apostles, who passed it on to the earliest Christians, the eucharist is once again recognized as the hub of Christian life. But it always is more than remembrance of the Last Supper in the usual sense of fondly recalling a good time shared with friends. It is in actuality something that is referred to by Dix as an *anamnesis,* the recalling of an event in order to bring it alive in the present. Charles P. Price and Louis Weil in *Liturgy for Living* say that from the beginning the eucharist has

> enabled the company of faithful Christians to stand in that single, full moment of time, between the death of Jesus in the past and the fulfillment of God's purposes in the future. It was one of the chief ways in which the mystery of Christ became actual . . . The Lord was present at these meals. Through him, communion with God had been restored.[39]

The eucharist transcends time. So when we say, "Christ has

died, Christ is risen, Christ will come again,"[40] we join all God's people past, present, and future. Chronological time was set aside by Christ, and his people are one-beyond the limits of mortality. All of the life, death, and Resurrection of Jesus is made present in the eucharist itself and present to us when we receive his Body and Blood.

Chapter 4

A Special Kind of Visit

Pastoral or Sacramental?

THE PASTORAL MINISTRY OF THE CHURCH "proclaims God's reconciling love to the community through care for the sick, the grieving, the needy, and those in pain."[41] The church is a pastoral community that has a life of caring as the Body of Christ. As a Lay Eucharistic Minister, you are called to share in this pastoral ministry, to extend the pastoral care provided at the altar and by the community. But an LEM's particular ministry is not a strictly pastoral one as are the ministries of those trained as Lay Visitors, Lay Callers, or Stephen Ministers. Primarily, your ministry as an LEM is a sacramental one. Yours also is a sacramental ministry, because you bear the sacraments of the bread and wine as a part of your ministry. A Lay Eucharistic Minister balances these two different parts of his or her ministry, always keeping both in mind. You are present with a person as a bearer of the bread and wine on behalf of the community at large. But you also are a pastoral representative and should be prepared to act pastorally toward those you are visiting. This knowledge is just as important for you as is your knowledge about how to conduct the LEM service and administer the sacrament to the sick.

Three Aspects of Ministry

A Ministry of Presence

The most important aspect of your pastoral ministry is your ministry of presence. To be present to a person means to focus on that person and his or her needs, whether spoken or unspoken. It means to try to get past your own needs and concerns of the moment in order to minister with your whole self. This is hard and takes practice and concentration. It also is difficult to communicate to people that you are totally present for them. Imagine how much difference it makes to sick people to know that they have your full attention, that you are solely concerned for them and them only when you are visiting as an LEM. See how this is a reflection of God's total and undivided concern for them, too? This is very meaningful to those who are sick or infirm because they often feel cut off from the familiar support of the parish family. God is using you to share God's love and show God's concern and that of the community through your relationship to the people you visit as an LEM. "The Lay Eucharistic Ministry is a ministry of presence which affirms the presence of Jesus Christ in a very special, mysterious and wonderful way to those in pain and those apparently cut-off from His body, the Church."[42]

A Ministry of Healing

One of the most exciting pastoral aspects of your presence as a Lay Eucharistic Minister is the potential for healing that you bring, healing with the eucharist itself and with your own presence as the representative of the community. Healing means being made whole. In receiving the communion, people are nurtured, strengthened, renewed, and healed in every sort of infirmity. No one is beyond the healing power of God. The sacrament is a vehicle for God's healing through the Holy Spirit. In taking the Body and Blood of Christ to those who need an LEM, you are enabling God to work in unknown ways in their lives. This is one of the significances of the gift that you bring as an LEM.

A Ministry of Hope

Part of your pastoral ministry is also that of bringing hope to people. You are able to provide the sick and the infirm with a foretaste of the heavenly banquet as well as with a concrete reminder of the community's care and concern for them for their needs in this life.

> Receiving this tangible symbol of [God's] love and presence restores our vision, strengthens our faith, and assuages the pain which we experience in our own brokenness and the brokenness of the world . . . The consecrated bread and wine are a forceful, tangible reminder to these people that LEMs visit who often feel excluded from life, that God's love and presence is always with them. His care in their pain, discomfort, or loneliness is constant.[43]

Communicating with the Clergy

As an extension of the pastoral care of your community, it is important that you keep your clergy informed about the people you are visiting as an LEM. Many parishes have developed forms for reporting each LEM visit. On them, you can note any observations made during the time you spent with the parishioner.

This is discussed in chapter 6, "Visiting Day." Remain aware of the responses of the parish member and family who are present. Sometimes you will notice things that no one else has. For example, tension between the ill parishioner and a family member. Or perhaps the person has taken a turn for the worse or is more depressed or in better spirits than the last time you visited. Your communication is important in helping your parish clergy be better ministers, too. Remember that yours is not a substitute for the ministry of your parish clergy. Do not try to counsel or solve problems. If you become unsure of your role in any situation speak with your clergy supervisor.

Confidentiality

In your capacity as an LEM, you will have the opportunity to talk with parishioners on a very deep level. Because illness makes many feel vulnerable and afraid, sick people often share things that are troubling them—things done in the past that they feel guilty about, family secrets long buried, life stories of triumph and failure. These things are told to you in confidence, and it is necessary to keep them strictly to yourself. Breach of this trust is inexcusable and can cause great harm, not only to that parishioners reputation and family but also to your parish family and to you. You must guard your tongue and keep these things confidential. If you know you are not the sort of person who can do this, you should not accept the responsibility of being a Lay Eucharistic Minister. Keeping these confidences also means that you will not initiate discussion of them on subsequent visits to the same person. *The Book of Common Prayer* admonishes those who have heard confessions: "The content of a confession is not normally a matter of subsequent discussion. The secrecy of a confession is morally absolute for the confessor, and must under no circumstances be broken."[44] Although LEMs do not usually hear confessions in the ritual sense, this is good advice for you, too.

Of course, you must use your discretion about sharing any of these confidences with your parish clergy, who also are bound to secrecy. Often it can be very helpful for them to know specifically what might be bothering a sick member of the parish. For instance, if you feel that the ill parishioner would benefit from talking to an ordained person, mention that in your report of the visit or make a special call to your clergy supervisor.

LEMs Receive, Too

One of the greatest rewards for being an LEM is that you discover that those to whom you minister are also ministering to you. Sometimes this takes new LEMs by surprise. People who are sick or infirm, however, often have valuable insights about life and faith to share with those who have their health. They have had to learn lessons in vulnerability and fear that many people who are well have not faced. As a part of your ministry of presence, listen to the wisdom of those you visit. Give care to them but do not take care of them. This can put them into a needy role and rob them of full participation with Christ in their own healing.

Chapter 5

Preparing Yourself To Be a
Lay Eucharistic Minister

Your Spiritual Life

THE MOST IMPORTANT PART of your preparation for Lay Eucharistic Ministry is your faithfulness in your own relationship to God. That faithfulness is expressed and built through personal and corporate prayer and study, as well as through your own participation in the Holy Eucharist. Some dioceses, such as Central New York even suggest that Lay Eucharistic Ministers maintain a relationship with a spiritual director or counselor in order to enrich their ministries to the sick as well as to enrich their own lives and spiritual journeys. The Diocese of New York requires a rule of life, a discipline that Lay Eucharistic Ministers choose for themselves and try to maintain. The point is that part of your commitment to being a Lay Eucharistic Minister is that you will be intentional about your spiritual life, both in the parish and in your workplace.

A helpful way to do this is by keeping your own journal about your relationship with Christ and with the world. A journal also is a good place to record each of your visits as a Lay Eucharistic Minister and reflect on how you felt, how you feel that you connected with the other person, any difficulties you might have had, and any insights that came out of the visit. LEMs also should keep a file of their training notes and any handouts or other materials that they feel important for reference.

The Week Before You Visit

Your prayers this week should center around those you are going to visit Sunday after the service. Lift them and their families, friends, and caregivers in prayer before God, asking for God's healing grace in their lives. Pray also for yourself as an instrument of God in this ministry. Be as specific as you can in these prayers. The collect, psalm, and lessons appointed for the coming Sunday can provide plenty of material for study during the week. This will prepare you to discuss them with those you visit. Having a grasp of the readings also will help you follow the sermon and its themes, if you are going to give a summary to the person you are visiting.

Each time you function as an LEM, ask yourself, What do I want to share of myself with this person today? Note that the question is about sharing yourself, not sharing news or gossip or pleasantries. Sharing yourself means being attentive and present to those you are visiting, willing to join with them in their anxieties and pain and willing to share some of your own struggles and hope. It means that, if you are good at extemporaneous prayer, offer that. If you are a quiet person, offer that part of yourself that knows how to listen at a deep level. If you are a person gifted in praying for others' needs, offer your intercessions and let the people you are visiting know that you are doing this on their behalf. Which of the gifts God has given to you are you moved to offer to this person through your work as a Lay Eucharistic Minister? Remember that they, too, will offer you gifts of themselves.

The Appointment

The "Suggested Guidelines" for the LEM's rite put out by the church's Standing Liturgical Commission state that "the people to whom Holy Communion is to be administered are to be noti-

fied in advance and the time of the appointment clearly set."[45]
This instruction stresses the seriousness of this ministry and the
fact that each visit is more than a drop-in social affair. Each
parish needs to develop its own system for making these appointments, and as an LEM, you should be familiar with the way it is
done at your church. In some places a church secretary makes the
appointments, in others it is left to the LEMS. Find out as soon
as possible whom you will visit the following Sunday. Knowing
the names of the ill and infirm persons and a little bit about their
situations can vastly enrich your personal prayers during the
week. This information also can help you anticipate how much
the person you are visiting will be able to take part in the service,
whom you should invite to accompany you on the visit, and if you
should adjust the service length to allow for a very ill or infirm
person. Know what parts of the service are optional and do some
thinking about these things before you go on each visit. But
many times circumstances can force a change in your plans—for
instance, if the person is more ill than you were led to believe or if
the person is more responsive than you anticipated.

When the appointment is made, many parishes give a simple set of instructions on what should be available for the LEM's
visit, i.e., suggestions regarding the size and height of the table
for the bread and wine. The Diocese of Arizona suggests that
when making the appointment, if possible, give the person to be
visited and their family and friends the list of the readings,
psalm, and collect for the Sunday. This is done so that before
the visit, they are able to be attentive to the service at the same
time that it is taking place in the congregation.

Inviting Others

In developing its rite for LEMS, the church's Standing Liturgical

Commission stressed the importance of taking others on the visit to underline the link between the congregation's worship service and the LEM's visit." Therefore, plan to invite in advance those who will go with you. Some Roman Catholic churches have eucharistic families—whole families that visit and participate in the service at the home or hospital and develop a relationship with the infirm person. Other suggestions are to take other LEMS, members of your own family, or relatives of the family of the person you are visiting. Also, members of the Sunday school youth group, particular friends of the ill or infirm person, or a fellow member of a church organization to which the person belongs—ECW, choir, or altar guild—could be invited. Your training in pastoral care will be valuable in assessing the most appropriate people to invite on each visit. Children and youth often are wonderful visitors, but in some cases it may not be a good idea to take them. Likewise, a person's relatives also can cause problems on the visit if there is tension in the family.

The Kit

The Lay Eucharistic Ministers' kit should contain the following:

>   a cruet: a vessel with a top, for carrying wine
>
>   a pyx: a small box for carrying the bread or wafers
>
>   a paten: a plate for serving the bread or wafers (optional)
>
>   a chalice: a cup from which to administer the wine
>
>   a corporal: a linen used beneath the vessels when setting
>   the Lord's Table

> purificators: the linens used to wipe the chalice after each person has drunk
>
> an intinction spoon: a small spoon (optional)

A cruet with a screw-on cap or a cork will allow you to carry the consecrated wine and water mixture without spilling. The communion bread or wafers usually are carried in a *pyx,* which is the Greek word for "box," and can be served directly from the *pyx* if you do not choose to carry a paten. The corporal may be used at more than one visit if it is not too stained. However, for sanitary reasons, a clean purificator should be used at each separate LEM visit. An intinction spoon can help you give communion to a very ill or comatose person. Often an old demitasse spoon is used.

The kit you will take on your LEM visits usually is modeled on the types of kits ordained clergy take when visiting the ill and infirm, though it need not be one of those. Your clergy will decide what sort of kit will be carried by the LEMs in your parish. The simplest thing to use probably is the kind of kit parish clergy usually use, and LEM kits also are commercially available. Augsburg Fortress has a pewter kit perfect for Lay Eucharistic Ministers that costs about $90. Almy offers an upscale silver-plated option at about $300. (See page 84 for ordering information.)[47]

When deciding what to use, however, attention must be paid to preserving the dignity of the sacrament. Some people feel that the communion kits manufactured to transport the eucharist to homes and hospitals do not provide vessels large enough to do proper reverence to the eucharist. Many contain a tiny chalice and a tiny paten that some say are too small to handle and look a bit as if the minister and recipients are "playing church."

What To Take

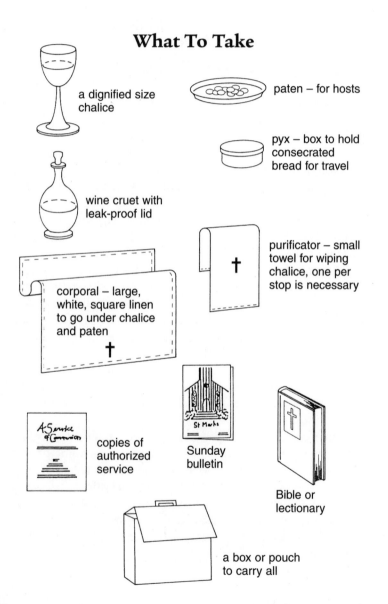

a dignified size chalice

paten – for hosts

pyx – box to hold consecrated bread for travel

wine cruet with leak-proof lid

purificator – small towel for wiping chalice, one per stop is necessary

corporal – large, white, square linen to go under chalice and paten

copies of authorized service

Sunday bulletin

Bible or lectionary

a box or pouch to carry all

The Set Up For Communion:
Two Options

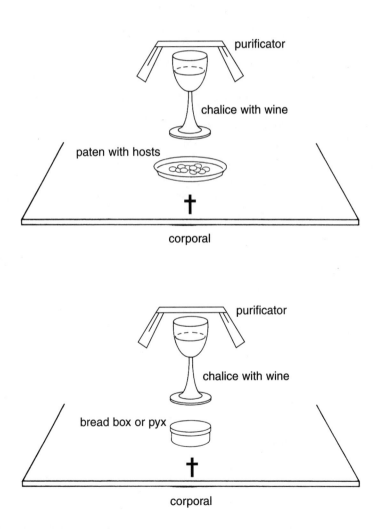

purificator

chalice with wine

paten with hosts

✝

corporal

purificator

chalice with wine

bread box or pyx

✝

corporal

Consideration should be given to creating a kit using vessels of larger size than those in home communion kits. Sometimes a chalice can be purchased that is the same design but a scaled-down version of one used in regular Sunday eucharist. Using a chalice that is nearly the size of the one usually seen in the parish eucharist can mean a lot to ill parishioners used to seeing a large one. If your parish wants to make its own kit, a block of styrofoam can be cut to allow your vessels to fit snugly in a small case.

Although some dioceses have used medicine bottles and pill boxes to carry the bread and the wine, these do not meet the criteria of dignified treatment of the sacrament.

The clergy in your parish should teach you how to set up the vessels, administer the eucharist, and clean the kit after each visit. You will be more confident on your first visits if you can practice with the kit that you will be using. The vessels should be handled reverently and not used for any purpose other than administering the eucharist.

After the Visit

Pause and reflect a few minutes on what you have done, giving thanks for the privilege and asking for awareness of how God has been using you in this ministry. The following week make some entries in your journal about your feelings and experience. Most importantly, continue to remember in your daily prayers those you have visited as an LEM, allowing God's love to penetrate you and them with its healing presence.

Support Group

Many dioceses suggest that their LEMs form support groups

where those participating in this ministry can gather to talk openly about their feelings, problems, and the situations that they are encountering. Often the LEMs in one parish meet together once a month or once every several months with the LEM clergy supervisor in the congregation. In other areas, the LEMs from smaller parishes also are banding together to support each other in this ministry. Many congregations feel it is important that their LEMs gather for a social occasion once or twice a year, too. This ministry sometimes can be as difficult as it is rewarding. Ongoing support from others who are encountering the same types of situations often can provide new insights and suggestions to improve your ministry and encourage your growth in Christ.

Chapter 6

Visiting Day

Before the Service

KITS MAY BE PREPARED by various people at various times. In some churches, the Altar Guild has that responsibility before the service. In that case, guild members on duty must know the number of kits needed for a given Sunday. In other places, each LEM is given the responsibility of preparing his or her own kit as needed. Remember that only one cruet is needed because the unconsecrated wine and water will be pre-mixed (if your parish uses water with the wine). It has been found that wine weakened with a good bit of water is more tolerable to those who are sick than is strong wine.

It works best logistically if the kits are prepared with unconsecrated elements ahead of time, assembled and placed on the altar to be consecrated at the same time as the elements during the service. Mixing and pouring at the table after everything has been consecrated is a very messy job and takes a lot of time because of the small cruets in LEM kits.

During Worship in the Church

The guidelines for the Lay Eucharistic Ministers' rite stress that the names of the people that you will be visiting be included in the congregation's "Prayers of the People" during the preceding church service.[48] This links the ill and infirm members, who have to be absent, to their parish family in a very close manner. If the people who will be visited have not been prayed for during the "Prayers of the People," they should be prayed for immediately before the LEMs are sent out. Be sure to tell each person you visit that he or she was prayed for by name in church that day.

During the service also hold yourself up in prayer that Christ will use you to be an able Lay Eucharistic Minister to the glory of God and the service of the gospel.

Being Sent Forth

The Standing Liturgical Commission has suggested the following be said by the priest to send forth LEMs after the service:

> In the name of this congregation,
> I send you forth bearing these holy
> gifts, that those to whom you go
> may share with us in the communion
> of Christ's body and blood. We who
> are many are one body, because we
> all share one bread, one cup.[49]

Several dioceses, including Colorado, also have developed their own forms for this (see appendix 6).

Dioceses differ on when parishes send their LEMs forth. Some want the LEMs to come forward during the ablutions, meaning that everyone in the congregation has taken communion, and the eucharistic vessels are being cleaned and put away by one priest or deacon while another is sending the LEMs forth. Or in a small church with only one clergy member, LEMs are sent immediately before or after the ablutions. It can be a powerful moment when LEMs move to the front to receive their kits while the congregation is kneeling in anticipation of the thanksgiving prayer. As the LEMs go from the church week after week, parishioners are reminded about the importance and availability of this ministry should they or a family member need it. Other churches send their LEMs out after the congregational prayer of thanksgiving on page 339 or on pages 365 and 366 of *The Book of Common Prayer* and before the blessing (if any) and the dismissal. Much of the drama and symbolism is lost if LEMs join the processional out of church at the close of the service. The idea should be clear that LEMs complete the service elsewhere.

The Standing Liturgical Commission directs that the sacrament be taken from the service by the LEM and administered to the ill and infirm members of the congregation "directly following"[50] or "immediately after"[51] the community's celebration of the eucharist. Dioceses have interpreted these directions in various ways. In some, the LEM goes directly from the service to the visit. In others, he or she goes after coffee hour and/or Sunday school. This practice, however, very much takes away from the theological significance of the LEM taking the sacrament from the priest's hand and then going directly from the church to sick and infirm members of the community. Taking the bread and wine immediately from the corporate worship affirms the integral relationship of the individual Christian to the Body of Christ. Each person who receives, whether in church or at home or in a hospital, participates in the corporate worship and is included as an important member of the family of God. The continuity between the congregation and the shut-in is both real and symbolic. The absent members are joined as closely as possible in sacred time and in chronological time to the primary eucharistic life of their congregation. When the sacrament is taken directly from the service, the dismissal also takes on a deeper sacramental meaning—the parish can see itself in the LEM's action of going forth to the larger congregation.

What to Wear

In most dioceses, a Lay Eucharistic Minister does not wear liturgical garments, such as a cassock and surplice or an alb, when making visits. This is to stress most strongly the LEM's link with the laity of the congregation. The clothes that you regularly wear to church are the most appropriate attire for an LEM, and they should be dignified enough to signal the seriousness of the visit. Some parishes also provide their LEMs with pins or crosses or medallions or name tags to wear when performing this ministry and to identify a person who might be a stranger.

What to Take

Besides your LEM kit and copies of the LEM service to enable others to participate, there are a variety of items that you could take to each LEM visit. A copy of that week's service bulletin that includes all the activities of the parish and lists what the Sunday worship was like is particularly helpful in making the absent member feel a part of things. In some parishes, cards are made for the ill by the Sunday school children. Others take a copy of the sermon to leave at the bedside, along with a copy of the LEM service, so that the sick or infirm member can go over them later. Anything that connects the person with the parish family usually is greatly appreciated. Other suggestions are flowers from your own garden or a tract or devotional guide like *Forward Day by Day* or *Journey through the Word*.

Make sure to double check the contents of your kit before leaving the church property. This heads off rude surprises!

Setting Up

Remember that you are a guest in another person's private space. Whether you are in a home, hospital or nursing facility, be as thoughtful as you would be in a friend's house.

In this person's private space, you are going to have to prepare a sacred space. Ideally, you should have a sturdy table of medium height with enough room on which to handle the vessels. If the table is not set up when you arrive, suggest something already in the room. A bedside table often will do nicely. If nothing in the room seems appropriate, ask for another table to be brought. To give the eucharist the dignity and reverence it deserves, the table should be completely cleared and clean. Clear it and wipe it off yourself, if necessary. Some dioceses suggest using candles and flowers. That, however, may complicate things unnecessarily for elderly parishioners, unless a family member or friend wants to take that responsibility. It should not be something that you, as a Lay Eucharistic Minister, should have to worry about. The eucharist should be your focus and the focus of everyone else present.

May LEMs have found that having a premade sign on the door of a hospital room or nursing home room—"Worship Service in Progress"— can cut down on interruptions during the service. Another idea would be to turn off the ringer on the phone or take it off the hook. If people do walk in during the service, ask them to join you or to wait outside.

Before You Start

Set up the table, pour the wine and water mixture in the chalice and put out the right amount of bread before you begin the service, so as not to break up the flow once you have started. You may do the service either standing or sitting. A general rule of thumb is to be on the same level as the person you are visiting. Instruct the others present whether they should stand or sit; do not leave it to them to try to decide what is best. Make sure that you have enough room to move around to administer the eucharist to all present. If visitors are standing or sitting on the far side of a bed, ask them to move out so that you will have unimpeded access to everyone. The most important thing before beginning the rite is to take the time to be reverent and fully present to God and to others. Do not rush! Most dioceses limit the number of visits that an LEM makes on a particular Sunday to two or three, so that the person does not feel rushed into keeping many appointments. One visit per Sunday is ideal. Your anxiety can be contagious. If you hurry, you give the message that those present are not important enough to merit your time and full attention. If necessary, before you start, briefly go over the service—what is their part, what is your part—so that participants will feel more at ease. Announce that you are ready to begin, wait for things to quiet as much as possible, take a deep breath, say a silent prayer asking God to use you through this ministry, and begin the rite.

Cleaning Up

The communion vessels should be cleaned after you have concluded the liturgy, so that the flow and focus of the service will not be interrupted. Follow the directions of your diocese and clergy supervisor for disposing of any leftover bread and/or wine (remember that it will have been consecrated) and for cleaning, storing, and returning the vessels to the church. The "Suggested Guidelines" of the national church say, "The container is to be returned immediately to the parish along with any unconsumed elements" (see appendix 4). Dioceses and parishes, however, have interpreted this differently because of local situations. Some Lay Eucharistic Ministers return to the church after completing their visits on Sunday, some return the kits the following day, and some return them any time before the next occasion they will be used.

Some LEMs are in charge of cleaning, maintaining, and preparing the kits they are going to use, but in other parishes the Altar Guild has that responsibility. The guidelines also state that "a suitable container in which to carry the two vessels for the bread and wine, corporals, and purificators is to be supplied." In other words, the Lay Eucharistic Minister is not expected to buy or own his or her own kit. The kit belongs to the parish, as does the work that the LEM has undertaken. In some cases though, LEMs and/or recipients of LEM ministries have wanted to give kits to the church as memorials or in thanksgiving for healing.

The Parish Register

Communions administered by the Lay Eucharistic Ministers should be recorded in the parish register. Ask your clergy supervisor how this should be done and by whom. Generally, LEM communions should be recorded under the category of "home communions," and you should note how many people were present, including yourself, and sign your name as the minister, along with any other notation your parish requires. Put the information in the book as soon as possible so that you do not forget. Some parishes get this information on a LEM report of the visit, and it is entered by a clergy person or secretary later.

Reporting to the Clergy

How this is done varies a great deal by diocese. In some dioceses, LEMs telephone their clergy to discuss each Sunday's visitation. But many dioceses have forms that the LEM completes after every visit. Copies then are given to the clergy and kept by the LEM for his or her records. A small preprinted card that fits inside the kit is handy and can be returned with the kit after the visit. Some of the forms are very simple, requiring only the information found in the parish register. Others require indepth reflection on each visit—what you learned, what you said, mistakes you made, how you felt, etc. Follow the directions of your supervising clergy and/or diocese. Certainly you should do some sort of self-examination after each visit, even if it is not required by the diocese or your parish. This is discussed in chapter 5, "Preparing Yourself to be a Lay Eucharistic Minister."

Chapter 7

The Service

About the Rite

I N JANUARY 1986, the Standing Liturgical Commission of the Episcopal Church issued a rite for Lay Eucharistic Ministers to use. It is entitled "Distribution of Holy Communion by Lay Eucharistic Ministers to Persons Who Are Ill or Infirm" (see appendix 1). Accompanying the rite were suggested guidelines for the use of the service (see appendix 4) and a short statement called "Concerning the Rite," which discusses the theology of Lay Eucharistic Ministry, the pertinent canon, and miscellaneous instructions on the use of the new LEMs' rite (see appendix 3).

This chapter will offer a general overview and a point-by-point discussion that includes theology, history, and practical pastoral advice for using the service. Of course, suggestions made here should not take the place of the directions of your diocese and clergy supervisor.

The church increasingly has become aware of the importance of the eucharist in the spiritual life of individuals and the church as a whole. It is as important to sense the mystery of the eucharist as it is to intellectually comprehend what the eucharist is about. As a Lay Eucharistic Minister, you have the responsibility to carry that sense of holy mystery and awe with you on your visits.

The rubrics, or italicized directions about a service in the Prayer Book and in the LEMs' rite, tell you how to do a service. They make the service smoother because they provide a clear explanation of what should be done when, so that the aura of worship is maintained and so that worshippers are not distracted. This helps enhance the eucharistic experience. But in doing the Lay Eucharistic Ministers' rite or any other service, you need to do more than just mechanically follow the rubrics. Sacramental experience is rooted more deeply than in just the proper way to carry out certain actions. God's grace is communicated through peoples' signs and actions. You, as a minister of the sacrament, should be aware of the tone of your voice, your bearing, your friendliness, your reverence to Word and Sacrament, and your ability to convey the parish community's love and concern to those you are visiting. All these attributes will contribute to the quality of your ministry. Keep in mind that you are bearing holy things for holy people.

The Lay Eucharistic Ministers' rite developed by the Standing Liturgical Commission is a service in contemporary English similar to that of the Rite II eucharist (see appendix 1 or *Book of Occasional Services 1994* page 53). A Rite I-type service (similar to that in the 1979 Prayer Book) has also been approved by the National Church's Liturgical Officer (see appendix 2). Many older parishioners being visited by LEMs are not as familiar with the contemporary language of the Prayer Book as they are with the older form, so the Rite I wording might be the best pastoral choice for them. If you choose to use a Rite I-type service, be aware of the language alterations required in the LEMs' rite. The necessary changes are discussed below. (A copy of this service is found in appendix 2.)

The diocese or your parish should provide copies of the service in both forms for you to take on your visits. The sheets should be printed clearly and in a type large enough for an elderly person to read.*

Laminating them helps them last longer. Forward Movement prints Rite II sheets with additional BCP prayers.

They can be ordered from 1-800-543-1813 at 45¢ per copy for large print and 15¢ per copy for regular print. By examining any service sheet, ill or infirm parishioners should be able immediately to tell which parts of the service require their responses and in which parts they may add their own thoughts and prayers aloud. Even so, it is often a good idea to briefly go over the service beforehand with a person you are visiting for the first time or one likely to forget between visits. It also helps sometimes to remind an elderly or confused parishioner about the purpose of your visit as soon as you get there, so that he or she knows what to expect and connects you with the congregation's worship.

---

* *A well-done large-print service is available in pamphlet form from Forward Movement Publications, 412 Sycamore Street, Cincinnati, Ohio 45202-4195 at 45¢ per copy for large print (Title #1071) and 15¢ per copy for regular print (Title #951).*

The Elements of the Rite

The Lay Eucharistic Minister greets the people.
The Peace of the Lord be always with you.

   Response *And also with you.*

Appropriately, the service begins with the peace, which already has been shared during the congregational worship service by the Lay Eucharistic Minister and perhaps by other people accompanying him or her on the visit. Now they have come to share that same peace of the Lord with the ill or infirm parishioner. The peace is an ancient greeting of the church, often used when entering the home of a fellow Christian. From written evidence of very early services of the eucharist, we also know that, as in this service for Lay Eucharistic Ministers, the liturgy began with the peace. Only later were prayers and hymns added to the start of the eucharist to set the stage for bringing the clergy and people together. The peace is used in this Lay Eucharistic Ministers' service as a symbol of the extension of the congregation's worship as well as a link with the earliest Christians who carried the sacrament to their ill and infirm members.

If you wish to use the LEM service in Rite I-type language, the response to the greeting becomes "And with thy spirit."

COLLECT OF THE DAY

Special collects (pronounced coll´-ects) are written for every Sunday of the church year, as well as for other major holy days, like saints' days. These prayers express the theme of each day in a particular form. If you read several collects, their structure becomes apparent. The collects mark sacred time, which is not the same as everyday or chronological time. They tell you and the person you are visiting as a Lay Eucharistic Minister that this Sunday is a special one, as are all Sundays in the church year. Each Sunday is the anniversary of Christ's rising from the dead. It is sacred time.

GOSPEL OF THE DAY, or some other passage of Scripture appropriate to the occasion.

The gospel reading also is a link with sacred time. It is taken from a lectionary used by the Episcopal Church, which provides different scriptural readings for each day in the church year. The Sunday readings run in three-year cycles. Like the collects the gospel points to the specialness of each particular Sunday. If you decide to read the gospel introduce it with these words: "A reading from the gospel of _____." The introduction of the gospel that you hear during the parish eucharist, "The Holy Gospel of our Lord Jesus Christ according to _____" is used only in worship in the church. The conclusion, "The Gospel of the Lord," also is used only in a congregational service. When you, as a Lay Eucharistic Minister, finish reading the gospel, you should conclude with "Here ends the reading" (which requires no response from the listener) or "The word of the Lord," (which calls for the listener to say, "Thanks be to God"). The ending you choose should be contingent on the ability of the person to respond.

Often churches print the scripture readings in the Sunday bulletin. If the person you are visiting is able to participate, invite him or her to silently follow along in the bulletin or in a Bible as you read it. Depending on the circumstances of the illness, the person to whom you are ministering could be invited to read aloud the gospel or another lesson, much as a Lay Reader does in church. As far as Lay Eucharistic Ministry is concerned, the greater the participation on the part of the person you are visiting, the better. For an alert parishioner who is ill or infirm, being included as much as possible in the service at home or in the hospital or nursing home, links her or him even closer to the corporate worship of the community.

It is best to stick with the scriptures because they are what has been read in the parish eucharist earlier that day. For the person hearing them, as well as for you, they will provide a clear link with that service. However, other readings such as poems, the words to hymns, and even secular writings are permitted in this LEMs' rite. Be very sure that what you use is appropriate. In many dioceses, changes and additions are not allowed at all or only with the permission of your clergy supervisor.

Comments may be made about the sermon of that day.

In this section of the service, you have the opportunity to summarize the points of the day's church sermon for the person you are visiting. If you are going to do this, it is crucial to pay close attention during the sermon and even take notes. Your job is not to critique the sermon of the preacher but to summarize his or her points. Some dioceses require that any comments on the sermon be developed in advance in dialogue with supervising clergy.

For some Lay Eucharistic Ministers, this portion of the service may be the most intimidating. Please note that it is an optional section, and if you feel uncomfortable including it, speak to your clergy supervisor. The Diocese of Montana makes a useful suggestion to its Lay Eucharistic Ministers to include a taped message from the preacher and/or some taped music from the service. Another suggestion, from North Dakota, is that the Lay Eucharistic Minister give a commentary on the gospel reading rather than a sermon synopsis. Of course, usually the Sunday sermon deals with the gospel appointed for that day, but you might prefer to stress something different from what the preacher said. Also, you can find appropriate and brief commentaries in publications like *Forward Day by Day*, but you should consult your clergy supervisor before using such resources.

If the person to whom you are ministering is able and willing, it might be good to engage him or her in a brief dialogue about the gospel or the other readings. Again, this is a way of including people and showing them that their views and feelings about the scriptures are valuable.

Suitable prayers may be offered.

Planning what you want to pray about is important and you should prepare for this element of the service before you visit. You may already be aware of the person's situation and have consulted with the clergy about him or her. However, use the time before you start the service to find out what that person says he or she feels concerned about. Be aware of any unvoiced concerns that you perceive, too, and include them in your prayers. You may offer prayers from *The Book of Common Prayer*, (a collection of them begins on page 810), or from any other source, or pray extemporaneously. Ask before you start what that person would like to have you offer in prayer. Then be specific in your prayers, calling by name the ill or infirm person and any others for whom you pray. If the parishioner to whom you are ministering wishes to and is able to, ask that person to offer his or her prayers aloud or silently. Encourage any other people present to do likewise. This time of prayer in the rite is a corporate experience, and it is important that you include people in any way they feel comfortable. This part of the service also is closely linked with the prayers for the sick or infirm person that have been offered in the earlier eucharist in the church. You will want to mention that the congregation prayed especially for the person you are visiting. In church the celebrant of the eucharist ends the "Prayers of the People" with a collect. You, too, might want to end this time of prayer that way. Suggested collects to conclude the prayers are found in appendix 5.

A Confession of Sin may be said.

Minister and People
> *Most merciful God,*
> *we confess that we have sinned against you*
> *in thought, word, and deed,*
> *by what we have done,*
> *and by what we have left undone.*
> *We have not loved you with our whole heart;*
> *we have not loved our neighbors as ourselves.*
> *We are truly sorry and we humbly repent.*
> *For the sake of your Son Jesus Christ,*
> *have mercy on us and forgive us;*
> *that we may delight in your will,*
> *and walk in your ways,*
> *to the glory of your Name.* AMEN.

The confession in this rite is optional, as is the confession in the Rite I and Rite II eucharists. In the 1928 *Book of Common Prayer,* however, the confession was mandatory. Therefore, some people, especially elderly people, may expect to join in a confession before they receive communion. As a Lay Eucharistic

Minister, make your own judgment about whether to include it. Some factors to consider are the age of the person you are visiting, the practice of your parish (do you routinely use the confession?), and the emotional and physical state of the person. If he or she seems especially anxious or troubled, even if you do not know the reason, it might be a good idea to include the confession and the subsequent declaration of forgiveness. You can also ask the person to whom you are ministering if he or she would like the confession. Keep in mind that this part of the service has great potential for healing. Confessing sins together, with the person to whom you are ministering, as well as with others present, is a powerful emotional symbol of our common humanity and a very personal experience of sharing.

The confession used in this Lay Eucharistic Ministers' rite is the same one used in the Rite II eucharist. Dioceses that have developed what they call a Rite I-form of this Lay Eucharistic Ministers' rite use the confessions on page 331 of the Prayer Book. The first confession on the top of the page, which is familiar to many older Episcopalians, is the same one found in the 1928 book. The second confession on page 331 is much like the confession in the Lay Eucharistic Ministers' rite seen above but in Rite I-style of language.

Minister

May Almighty God in mercy receive our confession of sorrow and of faith, strengthen us in all goodness, and by the power of the Holy Spirit keep us in eternal life. AMEN.

The Lay Eucharistic Minister declares forgiveness but does not absolve a person of sins. Absolution is a responsibility given to priests and bishops at ordination. By using "our confession" and "keep us in eternal life" in this Lay Eucharistic Ministers' rite, you are including yourself in it. Therefore, if a Rite I-form of confession is used, such as the ones found on page 331 of the Prayer Book, the Lay Eucharistic Minister must change the word you and your to the word us and our in the declaration of forgiveness on page 332. Of course, the declaration of forgiveness is never used without the confession.

THE LORD'S PRAYER

Although this service does not provide one, it might be a good idea to add a lead-in sentence to the Lord's Prayer. If you use the traditional wording of the Lord's Prayer, the lead-in sentence would be the one found on page 336 of the Prayer Book: "And now, as our Savior Christ hath [has] taught us, we are bold to say . . ." If you use the contemporary wording, the lead-in sentence would be the one found on page 363: "As our Savior Christ has taught us, we now pray . . ."

The version of the Lord's Prayer that you use should be chosen with care. Many older people are not familiar with the modern version. As in many of the variable elements of the Lay Eucharistic Ministers' service, one of the factors you have to consider in making the choice is what is familiar to the congregation and/or the person you are visiting.

ADMINISTRATION OF THE HOLY COMMUNION
(using one of the authorized words of administration)

Holy Communion is the climax of the service and should be administered carefully and reverently. It also may be the most difficult part for those who are very ill or aged. If you are awkward and unsure in this part of the service, you may lessen the experience of those receiving the Body and Blood of Christ.

Everyone at the service who is a baptized Christian should be invited to receive the eucharist, just as in most Episcopal Church services. This invitation is best issued before the service is begun, although polling people as to their baptismal status is not advised. Pastorally, it is better to err on the side of inclusivity. It is hoped that other people will be present, such as those you have brought from the parish service, nursing attendants, roommates, family members, and friends. These fellow Christians provide a visible and necessary link with the parish in particular and the whole Body of Christ in general.

It is usually good to ask a roommate in a semiprivate room to join you, particularly if he or she is not occupied with visitors. If so, or you desire more privacy, pull the curtain. People and their visitors are usually respectful.

Dioceses differ on whether the Lay Eucharistic Minister and people from the parish eucharist should receive communion only at the church, only on the visit, or at both. Receiving and administering Holy Communion, however, does provide a very graphic and symbolic link with the home parish. If you as the Lay Eucharistic Minister take the eucharist at the congregational service and then again at the visit, you will be reinforcing this link. Also, your own communion at the community service will have strengthened, nurtured, and renewed you before you were sent forth from the church. If you already have received, then you take that very recent spiritual renewal with you to your LEM visits that day.

If some ill people are able to take the eucharist in only one kind—either the bread or the wine—you should assure them that they have received full communion. Even if they cannot receive either element, continue the service and assure them that they are, indeed, a vital, loved part of Christ's Body.

If you have questions about how to administer the eucharist

to the person you are visiting, ask him or her directly either before the service or just before you administer the elements. Follow that person's suggestions or instructions to help him or her receive the Body and Blood. If the person or an attendant or relative cannot answer you, use your own judgment. If a person has mouth or nose tubes, ask medical attendants how this limits your administering the eucharist. An intinction spoon can be carried in your kit. Using the spoon, soak a bit of wafer in a drop or two of wine or just place a drop of wine into the very ill person's mouth.

Your clergy supervisor and the training you receive from your diocese and/or your supervisor should thoroughly cover the practical aspects of administering the eucharist in a home or hospital setting, because situations and local practice vary a great deal.

Many Lay Eucharistic Ministers have been Chalice Bearers or Liturgical LEMs at regular church eucharists and thus are familiar with handling the chalice. Some parishes, however, use Lay Eucharistic Minister kits in which the chalice is much smaller than the ones used in church. Practice with the vessels you will be using is an essential part of your training. Diagrams of the vessels and linens are in chapter 5 for you to review.

No matter how practiced or careful you are, accidents still happen. If the wine spills, wipe it up with the corporal if the purificator will not absorb it all. If a wafer falls, pick it up. Do not consume it because of sanitary reasons but put it into the kit to dispose of later. If you do not have enough wafers with you, break them in order to administer to everyone. People with communicable diseases should be given the cup after everyone else has partaken, otherwise intinct the wafer for them or ask them to intinct it for themselves. Intinction is the practice of dipping the wafer into the wine in the chance without wetting the fingers. In cases of communicable diseases, check with medical personnel before you enter the room to get instructions about washing your hands and the vessels in your kit, as well as about the necessity of wearing gowns and masks.

Generally, it does not matter who receives eucharist in what order, or if you receive it first or last. You probably would break the rhythm of the service, however, if you were to communicate yourself after several people and before the rest.

The "Words of Administration" are what you say when you give Holy Communion. The forms are as follows:

Contemporary form

The Body of Christ, the bread of heaven.
The Blood of Christ, the cup of salvation.

Abbreviated form

The Body (Blood) of our Lord Jesus Christ keep you in everlasting life.

> For intinction: The Body and Blood of our Lord Jesus
> Christ keep you in everlasting life.

Traditional form

The Body of our Lord Jesus Christ, which was given for thee, preserve thy body and soul unto everlasting life. Take and eat this in remembrance that Christ died for thee, and feed on him in thy heart by faith, with thanksgiving.

The Blood of our Lord Jesus Christ, which was shed for thee, preserve thy body and soul unto everlasting life. Drink this in remembrance that Christ's Blood was shed for thee, and be thankful.

You may use the contemporary form, the abbreviated form, or the traditional form. All three are found on page 338 of the Prayer Book in Rite I, although the contemporary form usually is used for Rite II eucharist. The traditional form might be more familiar to older parishioners but is quite a mouthful for an informal setting. Memorize the words you have chosen and speak them loudly enough for the communicant to hear, especially if he or she is elderly or if there is a noisy hospital environment.

Closing Prayer

Minister

> *O gracious God, whose Christ stretched out arms of love upon the hard wood of the cross to embrace all the peoples of the earth; We give you thanks for feeding <u>N</u>. our <u>sister</u> with the Sacrament of that precious Body and Blood, which is the sign and instrument of our common life, and also for enriching our parish family by <u>her</u> sharing with us the food of our pilgrimage, the foretaste of that heavenly banquet of which we shall partake with all your saints; through Jesus Christ, our Savior.* AMEN.

This prayer of thanksgiving should immediately follow the administration of the communion. Pray it before you clean up the vessels, personalizing it with the first name and gender of the person you are visiting. This thanksgiving echoes the words of one of the prayers for mission used at Morning Prayer as well as the postcommunion prayer of the parish's earlier eucharist. It brings together the theological themes of the Lay Eucharistic Ministers' service: the mystery of how the Body and Blood unite the faithful with Christ and with the world, and the concept that the service has been an extension of the congregation's eucharist. These themes graphically portray the importance of the ill or infirm member to the parish and link that person with the parish family.

Minister *Let us bless the Lord.*
Response *Thanks be to God.*

This ancient dismissal lets the people to whom you are ministering know that the service is over. Like all other parts of this Lay Eucharistic Ministers' rite, if you do not get a response from the person you are visiting, do not let it make you anxious or feel that you have failed. You may respond yourself. The person may be too ill or depressed to participate. It might help you to remember that no matter where people are in their silence, even if they are in a very deep coma, Christ's healing love can and does reach them. You are there to be a visible sign of that love.

Appendices

Appendix 1. Distribution of Holy Communion by lay Eucharistic Ministers to Persons Who Are Ill or Infirm
(Source: The Standing Liturgical Commission)

This form is to be used only immediately after a Celebration of the Holy Eucharist on Sunday or other regularly scheduled Celebrations.

The Lay Eucharistic Minister should be accompanied by other persons from the congregation.

The Lay Eucharistic Minister greets the people
> The Peace of the Lord be always with you.
> *Response*   And also with you.

Collect of the Day

Gospel of the Day, or some other passage of Scripture appropriate to the occasion.

Comments may be made about the sermon of that day.

Suitable prayers may be offered.

A Confession of Sin may be said
> *Most merciful God,*
> *we confess that we have sinned against you*

in thought, word, and deed,
by what we have done,
and by what we have left undone.
We have not loved you with our whole heart;
we have not loved our neighbors as ourselves.
We are truly sorry and we humbly repent.
For the sake of your Son Jesus Christ,
have mercy on us and forgive us;
that we may delight in your will,
and walk in your ways,
to the glory of your Name. Amen.

Minister   May Almighty God in mercy receive our confession of sorrow and of faith, strengthen us in all goodness, and by the power of the Holy Spirit keep us in eternal life. **AMEN**.

The Lord's Prayer

Administration of the Holy Communion
    (using one of the authorized words of administration)

Closing Prayer
    O gracious God, whose Christ stretched out arms of love upon the hard wood of the cross to embrace all the peoples of the earth: We give you thanks for feeding *N.* our *sister* with the Sacrament of the precious Body and Blood, which is the sign and instrument of our common life, and also for enriching our parish family by *her* sharing with us the food of our pilgrimage, the foretaste of that heavenly banquet of which we shall partake with all your saints, through Jesus Christ, our Savior. *Amen*.

Minister   Let us bless the Lord.
Response   Thanks be to God.

Appendix 2. Distribution of Holy Communion by Lay Eucharistic Ministers to Persons Who Are Ill or Infirmed— Rite I

(adaptation of Standing Liturgical Commission rite)

This form is to be used only immediately after a Celebration of the Holy Eucharist on Sunday or other regularly scheduled Celebrations.

The Lay Eucharistic Minister should be accompanied by other persons from the congregation.

The Lay Eucharistic Minister greets the people
          The Peace of the Lord be always with you.
    Response   And with thy spirit.

Collect of the Day

Gospel of the Day, or some other passage of Scripture appropriate to the occasion.

Comments may be made about the sermon of that day.

Suitable prayers may be offered.

A Confession of Sin may be said
     Almighty God,
     Father of our Lord Jesus Christ,
     maker of all things, judge of all men;
     We acknowledge and bewail our manifold sins and wickedness,
     which we from time to time most grievously have committed,
     by thought, word, and deed, against thy divine Majesty,
     provoking most justly thy wrath and indignation against us.
     We do earnestly repent,

and are heartily sorry for these our misdoings;
the remembrance of them is grievous unto us,
the burden of them is intolerable.
Have mercy upon us,
have mercy upon us, most merciful Father;
for thy Son our Lord Jesus Christ's sake,
forgive us all that is past;
and grant that we may ever hereafter
serve and please thee in newness of life,
to the honor and glory of thy Name;
through Jesus Christ our Lord. Amen.

Minister   Almighty God, our heavenly Father, who of his great mercy hath promised forgiveness of sins to all those who with hearty repentance and true faith turn unto him, have mercy upon us, pardon and deliver us from all our sins, confirm and strengthen us in all goodness, and bring us to everlasting life; through Jesus Christ our Lord. Amen.

The Lord's Prayer

Administration of the Holy Communion
     (using one of the authorized sentences of administration)

Closing Prayer
     O gracious God, whose Christ stretched out arms of love upon the hard wood of the cross to embrace all the peoples of the earth: We give thee thanks for feeding *N.* our *sister/brother* with the Sacrament of that precious Body and Blood, which is the sign and instrument of our common life, and also for enriching our parish family by *her/his* sharing with us the food of our pilgrimage, the

foretaste of that heavenly banquet of which we shall partake with all thy saints; through Jesus Christ our Lord. Amen.

Minister   Let us bless the Lord.
Response   Thanks be to God.

Appendix 3. Concerning the Rite
(Source: The Standing Liturgical Commission, adapted)

The Book of Common Prayer affirms the place of the Holy Eucharist as "the principal act of Christian worship on the Lord's Day and other major Feasts," and thus the foundation of the corporate prayer of the Church. As an act of the whole community of faith, the Eucharist is a summons to all the baptized to share in the table of the Lord. This form for the distribution of Holy Communion by licensed lay persons is intended to foster a corporate sense of the Eucharist among those who, by reason of illness or infirmity, are unable to be present in their church's assembly on Sunday or some other principal feast.

This service is to be conducted by a duly licensed person immediately following such parish celebrations of the Holy Eucharist. The General Convention (1988) has specified that "The Lay Eucharistic Minister shall have one or both of the following functions, as specified in the license."

a) Administering the elements at any Celebration of Holy Eucharist in the absence of a sufficient number of Priests or Deacons assisting the celebrant,

b) Directly following a Celebration of the Holy Eucharist on Sunday or other Principal Celebrations, taking the Sacrament consecrated at the Celebration to members of the Congregation who, by reason of illness or infirmity, were unable to be present at the Celebration."

It is desirable that other parishioners, relatives, and friends also be present to communicate with the person visited. Those so ministered to should also be visited regularly by the clergy of

the congregation. In this way, those who are unable to participate regularly in the worship of the eucharistic assembly may
nevertheless experience their relation to the community and
also join their personal faith and witness to that of their community. It is appropriate that the person be invited to join in
commenting on the Scripture and in offering suitable prayers
during the rite.

Appendix 4. Suggested Guidelines

(Source: The Standing Liturgical Commission)

1. Lay Eucharistic Ministers must be adult confirmed communicants in good standing, be carefully chosen and trained, and be especially licensed. A candidate is to be recommended by the cleric in charge of the congregation to the Bishop of the diocese to be licensed. "A license shall be given only at the request, and upon the recommendation, of the Member of the Clergy in charge of the Congregation in which the person will be serving. The license shall be issued for a period of time not to exceed three years and shall be revocable by the Bishop, or upon the request of the Member of the Clergy in charge of the congregation." (Title III Canon 3, Sec. 2a 1988.)

2. Where a deacon serves in a congregation, that minister should supervise the work of the Lay Eucharistic Ministers.

3. It is recommended that the person to be ministered to be prayed for specifically in the Prayers of the People by the Congregation on that day.

4. The administration of the Sacrament to the persons visited should take place immediately after the service in the church. Following the communion of the people, the Lay Eucharistic Ministers come forward and are commended for this ministry with the following or similar words:

> In the name of this congregation,
> I send you forth bearing these holy
> gifts, that those to whom you go
> may share with us in the communion
> of Christ's body and blood. We who
> are many are one body, because we
> all share one bread, one cup.

5. A suitable container in which to carry the two vessels for the bread and wine, corporals, and purificators is to be supplied. The container is to be returned immediately to the parish along with any unconsumed elements.

6. The people to whom Holy Communion is to be administered are to be notified in advance and the time of the appointment clearly set.

7. Only the order of the rite entitled *"Distribution of the Holy Communion by Lay Eucharistic Ministers"* is to be used.

Appendix 5. Suggested Prayers

(Source: Diocese of Oklahoma)

See the following from *The Book of Common Prayer*:
    Prayer for the Sick, page 208
    Prayers for the Sick, beginning page 458
    Prayer for the Human Family, page 815
    Prayer for the Mission of the Church, page 816
    Prayer for the Parish, page 817
    Prayer for the Right Use of God's Gifts, page 827
    Prayer for Families, page 828
    Prayer for Those Who Live Alone, page 829
    Prayer for the Aged, page 830
    Prayer for a Birthday, page 830
    Prayer for Those We Love, page 831
    Prayer for a Person in Trouble or Bereavement, page 831
    Prayer for Guidance, page 832
    Prayer for Quiet Confidence, page 832
    Prayer for Protection, page 832
    Prayer of General Thanksgiving, page 836

Appendix 6. Alternative Prayers for Sending Forth LEMs

(Source: Diocese of Colorado)

Celebrant: N. and N. we send you out to share Communion this week with N. N. and N. N.

People: May you carry the prayers of all of us as you take this sacrament of Christ's presence.

Celebrant: May those who receive it from you be strengthened and encouraged in that community we have together in our Lord Jesus Christ.

(Source: Diocese of Central Pennsylvania)

In the healing name of Jesus, and with the compassionate embrace of the family of St. John's, we send you forth bearing these Holy gifts of Our Lord's spiritual Body and Blood, that those to whom you go may experience with us the majesty and the mystery of his presence through the sharing of the wafer and the cup. May the one bread and the one wine call us into the binding awareness of our unity. Nothing, whether it be distance, illness, or age can ever separate us from the knowledge of our personal worth and our oneness in Jesus Christ our Lord. Amen.

(Source: Church of the Advent, Spartanburg, S.C.)

The Sending Forth

Celebrant: N. and N. we send you out to share this Holy Communion with N. N. and N. N. May those who receive it from you be strengthened and encouraged in that community we have together in our Lord Jesus Christ.

People: In the healing name of Jesus Christ, and with the compassionate embrace of the family of the Church of the Advent, we send you forth bearing these holy gifts of our Lord's spiritual body and blood. We pray that those to whom you go may experience with us the mystery of Christ's presence through the sharing of the wafer and the cup. May the *one* bread and *one* wine call us into awareness of *our unity* in the family of Christ.

Appendix 7. Various Rites of Commissioning of LEMs
(Source: Diocese of Delaware)

Sponsor: I present to you these persons who have been chosen and licensed to administer the Holy Communion in this congregation to the sick and the infirm.

Antiphon
The cup of blessing which we bless is a sharing in the Blood of Christ.
The bread which we break is a sharing in the Body of Christ.

Versicle: As often as you eat this bread and drink this cup:
Response: You proclaim the Lord's death until he comes.

Let us pray.

Grant, Almighty God, that those through whom the sick and infirm are included in the distribution of the Holy Communion may live in love and holiness according to your commandment, and at the last come to the joy of your heavenly feast with all your saints in light, through Jesus Christ our Lord. Amen.

In the Name of God and of this congregation, I commission you (N.) to share the Holy Communion with those prevented from attending the Parish Eucharist (and give you this _____ as a token of your ministry).

(Source: Diocese of Northern Indiana)

1. Persons authorized to distribute Holy Communion in special circumstances should be commissioned by the minister in charge of a congregation at a principal celebration.

2. Initially, the minister should address the reasons for this ministry in the context of a sermon, and those who are about to be commissioned should be prayed for during the Prayers of the People. At an appropriate time (e.g., before the Peace) in the celebration, those so chosen should come forward to the sanctuary and stand before the celebrant.

3. The suggested form:

Dear Friends in Christ,

Our brothers and sisters N. and N. are to be entrusted with the administration of the Holy Communion in the name of God and of this congregation to those who are unable to be present at principal Celebrations of the Eucharist.

N. and N., in this ministry, you must be examples of Christian living in faith and conduct; you must strive to grow in holiness through this sacrament of unity and love. Remember that, though we are many, we are one body because we share the one bread and one cup.

As ministers of Holy Communion be, therefore, especially observant of the Lord's command to love your neighbor. For when he gave his body as food to his disciples, he said to them "This is my commandment, that you should love one another as I have loved you."

The celebrant then asks them these questions:

Are you resolved to undertake the office of Lay Eucharistic Minister in order to build up Christ's Body, the Church?

Candidate **I am.**

Are you resolved to administer the Holy Communion with the utmost care and reverence?

Candidate **I am.**

The celebrant asks all to stand, and the candidates to kneel.

Dear Friends, let us pray with confidence to the Father; let us ask him to bestow his blessing on these persons chosen to be Lay Eucharistic Ministers.

(Pause for silence)

Almighty God, merciful Father, creator and redeemer of your family, bless our brothers and sisters N. and N. May they faithfully give the wonderful holy sacrament to your people. Strengthened by this sacrament, may they come at last to the heavenly banquet and stand with angels and archangels in adoration; through Jesus Christ our Lord, Amen.

(Source: Diocese of Central New York)

THE EXAMINATION

(The congregation being seated, the celebrant stands in full view of the people. The sponsors and candidates stand facing the celebrant.)

Celebrant

> Brothers and Sisters in Christ Jesus, we are all baptized by the one Spirit into one Body, and given gifts for a variety of ministries for the common good. Our purpose is to commission these persons in the Name of God and of this congregation to a special ministry to which they are called.

The celebrant asks the sponsors

> Are these persons you are to present prepared by a commitment to Christ as Lord, by regular attendance at worship, and by the knowledge of their duties, to exercise their ministry to the honor of God, and the well-being of his Church?

Sponsor

> **I believe they are.**

Celebrant

> You have been called to a ministry in this congregation. Will you, as long as you are engaged in this work, perform it with diligence?

Candidate

I will.

Celebrant

Will you faithfully and reverently execute the duties of your ministry to the honor of God, and the benefit of the members of this congregation?

Candidate

I will.

THE COMMISSIONING

(The appointed antiphons may be read or sung by all, or by the celebrant, or by some other person.)

Sponsor

I present to you these persons who have been chosen and licensed to administer the chalice in this congregation.

Antiphon

The cup of blessing which we bless is a sharing in the Blood of Christ. The bread which we break is a sharing in the Body of Christ.

Versicle.　　As often as you eat this bread and drink this cup:

Response.　　You proclaim the Lord's death until he comes.

Let us pray.　　(Silence)

Grant, Almighty God, that those who minister the cup of blessing may live in love and holiness according to your commandment, and at the last come to the joy of your heavenly feast with all your saints in light; through Jesus Christ our Lord. Amen.

In the Name of God and on behalf of O'Kelley Whitaker, Bishop of Central New York, and of his congregation, I commission you ___N___ to administer the chalice in your Parish when directed by your priest to take Communion to the ill and infirm. I give you this certificate as authorization of your ministry.

(Source: Diocese of Central Pennsylvania)

Before the Offertory of the Eucharist, the person(s) comes (come) forward at the invitation of the celebrant, and, standing before the congregation, makes (make) the Act of Commitment.

Celebrant: **Brothers and sisters in Christ Jesus, we are all baptized by the one Spirit into one Body, and given gifts for a variety of ministries for the common good. Our purpose is to commission this (these) person(s) in the Name of God and of this congregation to a special ministry to which he/she (they) is (are) called.**

The Celebrant then asks the candidate or candidates

Do you renounce Satan and all the spiritual forces of wickedness that rebel against God?

Answer: **I renounce them.**

Do you renounce the evil powers of this world which corrupt and destroy the creatures of God?

Answer: **I renounce them.**

Do you renounce all sinful desires that draw you from the love of God?

Answer: **I renounce them.**

Do you turn to Jesus Christ and accept him as your Savior?

Answer: **I do.**

Do you put your whole trust in his grace and love?

Answer: **I do.**

Do you promise to follow and obey him as your Lord?

Answer: **I do.**

Having been duly trained and licensed by The Bishop of The Diocese of Central Pennsylvania to perform the duties and responsibilities of the offices of Lay Reader and/or Lay Eucharistic Minister, will you as long as you are engaged in this work, perform it with diligence?

Answer: **I will.**

Will you faithfully and reverently execute the duties of your ministry to the honor of God and the benefit of the members of this congregation?

Answer: **I will.**

The Celebrant then addresses the congregation, saying

Will you who witness these promises do all in your power to support this (these) person(s) in his/her (their) performance of this special ministry in the life of our parish?

People: **We will.**

Antiphon said by all

There are varieties of gifts, but the same Spirit; and there are varieties of service, but the same Lord; and there are varieties of working, but it is the same God who inspires them all in everyone.

Celebrant: **Let the word of Christ dwell in you richly:**

People: **Do everything in the name of the Lord Jesus.**

Celebrant. **In the name of this congregation I commend you to this work, and pledge you our prayers, encouragement, and support.**

Let us pray.

Almighty God, look with favor upon this (these) person(s) who has (have) reaffirmed his/her (their) commitment to follow Christ and to serve in his name. Give him/her (them) courage, patience, and vision; and strengthen us all in our Christian vocation of witness to the world, and of service to others; through Jesus Christ our Lord. Amen.

Look with favor upon those whom you have called, O Lord, to be Lay Readers and Lay Eucharistic Ministers in your Church; and grant that he/she (they) may minister your Word and Sacraments with steadfast devotion, and by the constancy of his/her (their) faith and the innocency of his/her (their) life (lives) may adorn in all things the doctrine of Christ our Savior; who lives and reigns for ever and ever. Amen.

In the name of God and of this congregation, I commission you (N.) as Licensed Lay Reader and/or lay Eucharistic Minister (and give you this certificate as a symbol of your ministry) in this parish.

The service then continues with the exchange of the Peace and the Offertory.

The Peace

All Stand.   The Celebrant says to the people
The peace of the Lord be always with you.

People: And also with you.

The Ministers and People may greet one another in the name of the Lord.

Notes

1. General Convention of the Episcopal Church, *Constitution and Canons for the Episcopal Church* (New York: General Convention, 1988), p. 59. Hereafter referred to as *Canons* 1988.

2. Hippolytus, *The Apostolic Tradition of Hippolytus,* ed. Dom Gregory Dix (Harrisburg, PA: Morehouse Publishing, 1991), 26, p. 58.

3. Eusebius, *The History of the Church,* trans. G.A. Williamson (Middlesex, England: Penguin Books, 1986), pp. 284-85.

4. Melania the Younger, "Vita Sanctae Malaniae Junioris: Auctore Coaevo et Sanctae Familiar," *Analecta Bollandiana,* ed. Carolus De Smedt, Josephus de Backer, Carolus Houze, Franciscus Van Ortroy, and Josephus Van De Gheyn, 23 (1889): 16-63.

5. Gregory Nazianzen and Ambrose, *Funeral Orations,* trans. Leo P. McCauley, John J. Sullivan, Martin R.P. McGuire, and Roy J. Deferrari, Fathers of the Church, vol. 22 (New York: Fathers of the Church, 1953), pp. 161-259.

6. Jerome, *Saint Jerome Lettres: Belles Lettres,* ed. Jerome Labourt (1951), col. 11, p. 142.

7. Gregory the Great, *The Dialogues of Saint Gregory the Great*, ed. Edmund G. Gardner (London: Philip Lee Warner, 1911), II.37, p. 99.

8. Bede, the Venerable, *A History of the English Church and People,* trans. Leo Sherley-Price, 3d ed., revised by R.E. Latham (Harmondsworth, Middlesex, England: Penguin Books, 1982), IV, 24, pp. 250-53.

9. J.D. Mansi, ed., *Sacrorum Conciliorum nova et amplissima Collectio*, XI, co. 969, as cited by Nathan Mitchell, *Cult and Controversy: The Worship of the Eucharist Outside Mass*, Studies in the Reformed Rites of the Catholic Church, no. 4 (New York: Pueblo Publishing, 1982), P. 278.

10. Mansi, XI, cols. 1199-1200, as cited by Mitchell, *Cult and Controversy*, P. 278.

11. John T. McNeil and Helena M. Gamber, eds., trans., *Medieval Handbooks of Penance*, P. 224, as cited by Mitchell, *Cult and Controversy*, P. 272.

12. Mitchell, *Cult and Controversy*, p. 279.

13. WH. Freestone, *The Sacrament Reserved*, P. 228, as quoted in Mitchell, *Cult and Controversy*, P. 279.

14. J.H. Crehan, "Medieval Ordinations," *The Study of Liturgy*, ed. Cheslyn Jones, Geoffrey Wainwright and Edward Yarnold (New York: Oxford University Press, 1978). pp. 320-25.

15. J.P. Migne, ed., *Patrologia Latina*, 136, col. 560, as cited by Mitchell, *Cult and Controversy*, P. 279.

16. Freestone, *Sacrament Reserved*, P. 228, as quoted in Mitchell, *Cult and Controversy*, pp. 279-80.

17. Mitchell, *Cult and Controversy*, P. 280.

18. Frederick Maurice Powicke and C.R. Cheyney, eds., *Councils and Synods, with Other Documents Relating to the English Church*, I, P. 488, as quoted in Mitchell, *Cult and Controversy*, P. 280.

19. Mitchell, *Cult and Controversy*, P. 303.

20. J.C. Didier, "Le Ministre Extraordinaire de la Distribution de la Communion," *La Maison-Dieu* 103 (July 1970): 73-85.

21. Austin Flannery, ed., Vatican Council II. *The Conciliar and Post Conciliar Documents* (Northport, NY: Costello Publishing, 1975), P. 226.

22. Ibid., P. 227.

23. Richard McBrien, Church. *The Continuing Quest*, P. 33, as quoted in Mitchell, *Cult and Controversy*, P. 294.

24. Ernest A. Falardeau, "Special Ministers of Communion: Building the Church through Eucharistic Ministry," *The Priest* (June 1983): 18-20.

25. Diocese of Oklahoma, "New Ministries: Lay Eucharistic Visitors—An Introduction" (Handbook for Lay Eucharistic Visitors, Oklahoma City, OK: Diocese of Oklahoma, 1987), P. 3.

26. *The Book of Common Prayer* (New York: Church Hymnal Corp., 1979), P. 854. Hereafter referred to as *BCP* 1979.

27. Mitchell, *Cult and Controversy*, P. 302.

28. Ibid., P. 300.

29. *Canons* 1988, P. 59.

30. Ibid.

31. Falardeau, "Special Ministers of Communion," P. 20.

32. David N. Power, *Gifts That Differ: Lay Ministries Established and Unestablished*, Studies in the Reformed Rites of the Catholic Church, no. 8 (New York: Pueblo Publishing, 1980), P. 10.

33. Throughout this chapter, I am indebted to the work of Charles P. Price and Louis Weil, *Liturgy for Living*, Church's Teaching Series, no. 5 (New York: Seabury Press, 1979).

34. *BCP* 1979, pp. 323-32 and 355-60.

35. Dom Gregory Dix, *The Shape of the Liturgy*, 2nd ed. (New York and San Francisco: Harper and Row, 1982), P. 744.

36. *BCP* 1979, P. 13.

37. Ibid., P. 336.

38. J. Delorme, P. Benoit, J. Dupont, M.E. Boismard, and D.Mollat, *The Eucharist in the New Testament*, trans. E. M. Stewart (London: Geoffrey Chapman, 1964), p. 83.

39. Price and Weil, *Liturgy for Living*, p. 190.

40. *BCP* 1979, P. 363.

41. John N. Wall, Jr., *A New Dictionary for Episcopalians* (San Francisco: Harper & Row, 1985), P. 125.

42. Gregory M. Howe, "An Outline of Eucharistic Doctrine" (Position paper for the Diocese of Delaware, Wilmington, DE, 1986). P. 1.

43. Handouts from the Diocese of Central Pennsylvania.

44. *BCP* 1979, p. 446.

45. Standing Liturgical Commission of the Episcopal Church "Suggested Guidelines." Document accompanying the "Distribution of Holy Communion by Lay Eucharistic Ministers to Persons Who Are Ill or Infirm" (January 1986), p. 2. Hereafter referred to as SLC "Suggested Guidelines."

46. Standing Liturgical Commission of the Episcopal Church, "Concerning the Rite." Document accompanying the "Distribution of Holy Communion by Lay Eucharistic Ministers to Persons Who Are Ill or Infirm" (January 1986), p. 1. Hereafter referred to as SLC "Concerning the Rite."

47. A pewter Visitors Communion kit especially suitable for Lay Eucharistic Ministers is available from the Fortress Church Supply Store. For information call 1-800-FORTRES (367-8737). A pottery Communion kit is available from Altar Calling, 3275 South Race, Englewood, CO 80110.

48. SLC "Suggested Guidelines," p. 1.

49. Ibid.

50. *Canons* 1988, p. 59, and SLC "Concerning the Rite," P. 1.

51. Standing Liturgical Commission of the Episcopal Church, "Distribution of Holy Communion by Lay Eucharistic Ministers to Persons Who Are Ill or Infirm" (January 1986), p. 1; and SLC "Suggested Guidelines," p. 1.

Bibliography

Bede, the Venerable. *A History of the English Church and People*. Translated by Leo Sherley-Price. 3d ed., revised by R.E. Latham. Harmondsworth, Middlesex, England: Penguin Books, 1982.

The Bible. Revised Standard Version. Oxford Annotated Bible with Apocrypha. Edited by Herbert G. May and Bruce M. Metzger. New York: Oxford University Press, 1977.

The Book of Common Prayer. New York: Church Hymnal Corp., 1979.

The Book of Common Prayer, New York: Seabury Press, 1928.

The Book of Occasional Services, 2d ed., rev. New York: Church Hymnal Corp., 1988.

Buchanan, Colin. *What Did Cranmer Think He Was Doing?* Grove Liturgical Study, no. 7. 2d ed. Bramcote, Nottinghamshire, England: Grove Books, 1982.

Crehan, J. H. "Medieval Ordinations." In *The Study of Liturgy,* edited by Cheslyn Jones, Geoffrey Wainwright, and Edward Yarnold. New York: Oxford University Press, 1978.

Congar, Yves M.J. *Lay People in the Church: A Study for a Theology of Laity*. Translated by Donald Attwater. Revised ed. London: Geoffrey Chapman, 1985.

Davies, J.C., ed. *The New Westminster Dictionary of Liturgy and Worship*. Philadelphia: Westminster Press, 1986.

Delaplane, Margaret Ann. Episcopal Diocese of Delaware. Wilmington, DE Interview, 8 March 1989.

Delorme, J.; Benoit, P.; Dupont, J.; Boismard, M.E.; and Mollat, D. *The Eucharist in the New Testament.* Translated by E.M. Stewart. London: Geoffrey Chapman,1964.

Didier, J.C. "Le Ministre Extraordinaire de la Distribution de la Communion." *La Maison-Dieu* 103 (July 1970): 73-85.

Diocese of Central New York. *Handbook for Lay Eucharistic Ministers to Persons Who Are Ill and Infirm.* Syracuse, NY. Diocese of Central New York.

Diocese of Central Pennsylvania. Miscellaneous diocesan materials on Lay Eucharistic Ministers. Harrisburg, PA: Diocese of Central Pennsylvania.

Diocese of Colorado. "Guidelines for the Lay Eucharistic Minister." Denver CO: Diocese of Colorado.

Diocese of Northern Indiana. "Rite of Commission of Lay Eucharistic Ministers." South Bend, IN: Diocese of Northern Indiana.

Diocese of Oklahoma. "New Ministries: Lay Eucharistic Visitors—An Introduction." Handbook for Lay Eucharistic Visitors. Oklahoma City, OK: Diocese of Oklahoma, 1987.

Dix, Dom Gregory. *The Shape of the Liturgy.* 2d ed. New York and San Francisco: Harper and Row, 1982.

Eusebius. *The History of the Church.* Translated by G.A. Williamson. Middlesex, England: Penguin Books, 1986.

FaIardeau, Ernest A. "Special Ministers of Communion: Building the Church through Eucharistic Ministry." *The Priest* (June 1983): 18-20.

Farmer, David Hugh. *The Oxford Dictionary of Saints.* Oxford, England: Clarendon Press, 1978.

Flannery, Austin, ed. *Vatican Council II. The Conciliar and Post Conciliar Documents.* Northport, NY: Costello Publishing, 1975.

General Convention of the Episcopal Church. *The Blue Book: Reports of the Committees, Commissions, Boards, and Agencies of the General Convention of the Episcopal Church.* New York: General Convention, 1982.

General Convention of the Episcopal Church. *The Blue Book: Reports of the Committees, Commissions, Boards, and Agencies of the General Convention of the Episcopal Church.* New York: General Convention, 1985.

General Convention of the Episcopal Church. *The Blue Book: Reports of the Committees, Commissions, Boards, and Agencies of the General Convention of the Episcopal Church.* New York: General Convention, 1988.

General Convention of the Episcopal Church. *Constitution and Canons for the Episcopal Church.* New York: General Convention, 1985.

General Convention of the Episcopal Church. *Constitution and Canons for the Episcopal Church.* New York: General Convention, 1988.

General Convention of the Episcopal Church. *Journal of the General Convention of the Episcopal Church.* New York: General Convention, 1982.

General Convention of the Episcopal Church. *Journal of the General Convention of the Episcopal Church.* New York: General Convention, 1985.

Gregory Nazianzen and Ambrose. *Funeral Orations.* Translated by Leo P. McCauley, John J. SuMvan, Martin R.P. McGuire, and Roy J. Deferrari. Fathers of the Church, vol. 22. New York: Fathers of the Church, 1953.

Gregory the Great. *The Dialogues of Saint Gregory the Great.* Edited by Edmund G. Gardner. London: Phillip Lee Warner, 191 1.

Hatchett, Marion J. *Commentary on the American Prayer Book.* New York: Seabury Press, 198 1.

Hippolytus. *The Apostolic Tradition of Hippolytus.* ed. Dom Gregory Dix. Harrisburg, PA: Morehouse Publishing, 1991.

Howe, Gregory M. "Lay Eucharistic Ministry: An Historical Survey." Position paper, Diocese of Delaware, Wilmington, DE, 1986.

Howe, Gregory M. "An Outline of Eucharistic Doctrine.' Position paper, Diocese of Delaware, Wilmington, DE, 1986.

Jerome. *Saint Jerome Lettres: Belles Lettres.* Edited by Jerome Labourt, 1951.

Justin Martyr. "First Apology." In *Early Christian Fathers,* edited by Cyril C. Richardson. Library of Christian Classics, vol. 1. New York: Collier Books, 1970.

Lash, Nicholas, and Rhymer, Joseph. *The Christian Priesthood,* London: Darton, Longman & Todd, 1970.

Melania the Younger. "Vita Sanctae Malaniae Junioris: Auctore Coaevo et Sanctae Familiari." *Analecta Bollandiana.* Edited by Carolus De Smedt, Josephus de Backer, Carolus Houze, Franciscus Van Ortroy, and Josephus Van Den Chey. 23 (1889): 16-M.

MitchelL Nathan. Cult and Controversy: *The Worship of the Eucharist Outside Mass.* Studies in the Reformed Rites of the Catholic Church, no. 4. New York: Pueblo Publishing, 1982.

Power, David N. *Gifts That Differ. Lay Ministries Established and Unestablished.* Studies in the Reformed Rites of the Catholic Church, no. 8. New York: Pueblo Publishing, 1980.

Price, Charles P., and Weil, Louis. *Liturgy for Living.* Church's Teaching Series, no. 5. New York: Seabury Press, 1979.

Roache, Catharine Stewart. "The Communion." In *Images: Women in Transition.* Compiled by Janice Grana. Winona, MN: St. Mary's Press, 1977.

Seasoltz, R. Kevin, ed. *Living Bread, Saving Cup: Readings on the Eucharist.* Collegeville, MN: Liturgical Press, 1982.

Standing Liturgical Commission of the Episcopal Church. "Concerning the Rite." Document accompanying the "Distribution of Holy Communion by Lay Eucharistic Ministers to Persons Who Are Ill or Infirm," January 1986.

Standing Liturgical Commission of the Episcopal Church. "Distribution of Holy Communion by Lay Eucharistic Ministers to Persons Who Are Ill or Infirm," January 1986.

Standing Liturgical Commission of the Episcopal Church. "Suggested Guidelines." Document accompanying the "Distribution of Holy Communion by Lay Eucharistic Ministers to Persons Who Are Ill or Infirm," January 1986.

Wall, John N., Jr. *A New Dictionary for Episcopalians.* San Francisco: Harper & Row, 1985.

White, Edwin A. and Dykman, Jackson A. *Annotated Constitution and Canons for the Government of the Protestant Episcopal Church in the United States of America Otherwise Known as The Episcopal Church.* 3d ed., revision and updated by the Standing Commission on Constitution and Canons of the General Convention. New York: Office of the General Convention, 1981.

Whitmore, Hal. The Lay Eucharistic Ministers' Canon. M.Div. Honors thesis. The General Theological Seminary, New York, 1988.

Also used were numerous training materials from the following dioceses: Alaska, Arizona, Arkansas, Atlanta, California, Central Gulf Coast, Central New York, Central Pennsylvania, Colorado, Connecticut, Delaware, Eau Claire, East Tennessee, Eastern Oregon, Easton, El Camino Real Florida, Fond du Lac, Fort Worth, Georgia, Hawaii, Indianapolis, Kentucky, Lexington, Long Island, Louisiana, Maine,, Maryland, Massachusetts, Michigan, Minnesota, Mississippi, Montana, New Hampshire, New York North Dakota, Northeast Pennsylvania, Northern Indiana,

Northern Michigan, Northwest Texas, Northwestern Pennsylvania, Oklahoma, Quincy, Rhode Island, Rochester, South Dakota, Southern Virginia, Southwestern Virginia, Springfield, Texas, Vermont, Virginia, Washington, West Tennessee, West Texas, Western Kansas, Western Louisiana, Western Massachusetts, and Western Oregon.